Change Processes
in the
Public Schools

The Center for the Advanced Study of Educational Administration at the University of Oregon is a national research and development center which is supported in part by funds from the United States Office of Education, Department of Health, Education, and Welfare. The opinions expressed in this publication do not necessarily reflect the position or policy of the Office of Education and no official endorsement by the Office of Education should be inferred.

Seminar on change process in PUBLIC SCHOOLS, Portland Or., 196

Change Processes
in the
Public Schools

RICHARD O. CARLSON
ART GALLAHER, JR.
MATTHEW B. MILES
ROLAND J. PELLEGRIN
EVERETT M. ROGERS

A publication of
THE CENTER FOR THE ADVANCED STUDY OF
EDUCATIONAL ADMINISTRATION

UNIVERSITY OF OREGON
Eugene, Oregon

First Printing, February, 1965
Second Printing, August, 1965
Third Printing, November, 1965
Fourth Printing, April, 1966
Fifth Printing, November, 1966
Sixth Printing, February, 1968
Seventh Printing, March, 1969
Eighth Printing, December, 1969
Ninth Printing, September, 1971

Printed in the United States of America
at the University of Oregon Press, Eugene, Oregon

Designed and edited by Joanne M. Kitchel

The text of this book is set in Janson type
on Simpson's eggshell text

Library of Congress Catalog Number 65-63432

Foreword

Organizations have careers in much the same sense that individuals have careers. In the tracing out of organizational careers, a number of changes can always be detected, even among the seemingly most stable organizations.

Change in organizations comes about in many ways. Some changes occur with the size of the organization and some changes occur with the maturation process. Also, organizational change results, sometimes dramatically but most often not, from the succession of people through key offices. Similarly, a kind of evolutionary change in organizations can be seen as they adapt to forces within or conditions of their environments. To some extent, changes of this order can be called "organizational drift" because they frequently go unnoticed by those who direct the affairs of an organization. The effect of these rather gradual changes are almost imperceptibly viewed over a short time span but sometimes loom large when the overall career of the organization is considered.

In addition to organizational change that might be characterized as drift, change comes about in organizations by design or deliberate plan. Being seemingly "self" conscious about ends to be achieved and means of achieving ends, organizations strive for survival, if not perfection, and seem constantly to be proposing and carrying out change plans. It is this latter type of change, *planned change*, which is treated in this publication.

This publication is a report of a seminar conducted with public school officials by the Center for the Advanced Study of Educational Administration at the University of Oregon. The seminar, considered a pilot venture, had as its main objective the enhancement of the school officials' understanding of the planned change processes and of their skills in carrying out planned change. In formulating the design of the seminar we were aided by members of the Committee on Inservice Education of the Oregon Association of School Administrators. Some changes in the order and nature of events were made while the seminar was in progress; these changes resulted from the almost continuous conversation with the consultants and other interested persons on the question, "How are things going?"

The seminar, held in Portland, Oregon in October, 1964, revolved around two major elements: (1) small group discussions of papers prepared for the seminar by four consulting social scientists, and (2) what were termed "clinic sessions." These sessions brought the school officials and the social scientists together in small groups where attention was given to specific change problems that had been, and were being encountered by the school officials. In advance of the clinic sessions, the school officials prepared memoranda of their specific problems.

All of the events of the seminar are not reported here, nor does the order of the contents of this publication follow the order of the seminar itself.[1]

The publication includes three of the four papers prepared for the seminar by the consulting social scientists—those by Matthew B. Miles, Art Gallaher, Jr., and Everett M. Rogers. Unfortunately we were unable to secure publication rights to the paper by James Q. Wilson and consequently his work does not appear here. The papers by Richard O. Carlson and Roland J. Pellegrin, although they were read during the seminar, were not part of the grist for the mill in the clinic and discussion sessions. It will be noted that the papers of these latter two contributors present different perspectives on planned change from those contained in the papers by the consultants and in the summaries of the group discussions.

The final section of this publication is a summary of the seminar itself which was made by Donald E. Tope at its concluding session.

Some financial aid for the seminar was provided by the National Institute of Mental Health of the Department of Health, Education, and Welfare. Our indebtedness extends also to the University Council for Educational Administration for the aid which was provided through its Executive Director, Jack Culbertson. Although they are unnamed here, many persons contributed a variety of talents to the task of the seminar and their efforts are gratefully acknowledged.

RICHARD O. CARLSON
KEITH GOLDHAMMER
Seminar Coordinators

February, 1965
UNIVERSITY OF OREGON, Eugene, Oregon

---

[1] Although absent from this publication, a discussion of *The Jackson County Story* was included in the seminar. This case study exists in published form and may be obtained from the Center for the Advanced Study of Educational Administration, University of Oregon. (*The Jackson County Story, A Case Study,* by Keith Goldhammer and Frank Farner. University of Oregon, Center for the Advanced Study of Educational Administration, 1964.)

[vi]

Contents

1

Barriers to Change
in
Public Schools

By
RICHARD O. CARLSON

Barriers to Change in Public Schools

RICHARD O. CARLSON
University of Oregon

A GOOD MANY people, reflecting on our times, suggest that we are in the advanced stages of a revolution in education. Some of them are even prepared to argue the point, and there is considerable evidence to support their case. There are, for example, at least ten national projects in science, eleven in mathematics, one in English, two in foreign languages and four in social sciences that are currently preparing curriculum materials and testing them in the schools. The federal government has given considerable financial support to this so-called revolution in education. Over 12 million dollars has been disbursed by the Cooperative Research Branch of the U.S. Office of Education since 1956 for research on the improvement of education. This, of course, represents a very small amount in comparison to the support for the improvement of education which has been provided by the National Science Foundation and Title III of the National Defense Education Act.

In spite of all of the current activity, it seems fair to say that there is quite widespread pessimism about the ability of public schools to make rapid and adequate adaptation to our fast changing times.

I am sure you have heard many times Paul Mort's fully publicized finding that it takes 50 years for the complete diffusion of an educational innovation which is destined to be fully accepted. I am sure, too, that you are well aware of the generalization that public educational institutions are painfully slow to change. You have, no doubt, marveled, as I have, at the tremendous change facility of other sections of our work world such as agriculture and medicine. Evidence of the ability of these enterprises to change is all around us and constantly forces its way to our attention.

Why is this the case? Why are educational systems reputed to be slow to change and medicine and agriculture quick to change? Could it be that there exists a greater need to change practices in medicine and farming than there is need to change educational practices? Is the practice of education so advanced and the practice of medicine and farming so primitive as to explain the diverse rates of adaptability? I think not.

[3]

Three Barriers to Change

1. The Absence of a Change Agent

Part of the explanation of the slow rate of change in public schools, according to many students of organizational change, lies with the absence of an institutionalized change agent position in public education. A *change agent*, for the purposes of my remarks, can be defined as a person who attempts to influence the adoption decisions in a direction he feels is desirable. He is a professional who has as his major function the advocacy and introduction of innovations into practice.

The county extension agent is well recognized as a change agent as far as farming practices are concerned. But who is it that performs a similar role for educational practice? What office in public education as we know it has responsibility for the advocacy of change? Does such a function rest in the apparatus of state departments of education? Does it rest in the office of the county school superintendent? The answer to these questions seems clearly to be no. By and large, county and state levels of public education take as their major function one of regulation.

If the change agent role is not imbedded in county or state levels of public education, then perhaps it lies in the local school district unit. It would seem difficult to make a case that local school districts have developed positions wherein the superintendent takes as his major function the advocacy of change.

It seems easy to conclude that the change agent counterpart of the county extension agent has no office in our public school enterprise. And, as has been indicated, many attribute the slowness of change in educational practices to the absence of a change agent.

Let us assume, as seems reasonable to me, that by default of others, the change advocate role must be taken by the local school system through the office of the superintendent. This would seem to be not only a fair assumption, but, in the marked instances of rapidly adapting school districts, to be a fair description of reality.

Right away this makes obvious a difficulty: whereas the change agent prototype of the county extension agent operates outside of and free from the farm unit he is attempting to change, the school superintendent as a change agent is a central part of the unit he must take as his change objective. Being in and of the organization, the function of change advocacy for the school superintendent is difficult because he frequently must prescribe the change of his own practices.

In the area of providing public schools with a change advocate, the state of New York must be seen as a leader. During the last few years, through the Commission of Education in New York, a series of studies have been conducted aimed at the development of a plan for "improving the process of educational change in the elementary and secondary schools of the state." The plan for managing change that these studies have developed is worth your attention and can be found in a monograph titled "Organizing New York State for Educational Change," which is published by the New York State Department of Education. In essence, the plan suggests that in order to deal effectively with the problem of change in school practices, three distinct and separate units must be established under the control of the Commissioner of Education of New York. One unit is a design unit where ideas are generated. The second unit has the task of evaluating the ideas flowing from the design unit. The third separate unit has as its function the development and dissemination of the practices which emanate from the other two agencies. The extent to which this plan is successful in improving the process of educational change in the schools of New York is, of course, still to be seen. Nevertheless, it is very encouraging to see the human talent and effort that is involved in the undertaking. And it is clear that the problem of establishing a viable change advocacy function among the many levels in our system of education is one of extreme importance and one for which we should recruit our best minds.

2. A Weak Knowledge Base

In addition to the lack of a change agent, schools are also handicapped in change activities by the weakness of the knowledge base about new educational practices. This is apparent when one contrasts the knowledge base about innovations which is available to the school superintendent with that which is available to the county extension agent. As you know, the county extension agent is backed by very extensive and practiced research, experiment, and devolment operations. He is in a much more favored position than is the school superintendent to judge the merits of the innovations he attempts to have adopted, and to demonstrate these merits to the acceptors. It is rare indeed when an educational innovation is backed by solid research. It is even rarer to find an educational innovation which has been fully developed and subjected to careful trial and experimentation. Thus, the school superintendent as a change agent must ordinarily do not only the work of the county extension agent but also the work of the agricultural experimental station. This is a job of large dimensions. But, as you know from first hand experience, it is a job which is very exciting and satisfying.

The future may be brighter on this point: the school administrator may be relieved of some of the burdens of being both a county extension agent and an agricultural experimental station. The federal government has within the last year established four large educational research and development centers, (at the Universities of Oregon, Pittsburgh, and Wisconsin, and at Harvard) and more centers will be established in the future.

These centers are charged with research, development and dissemination responsibilities and in this sense can be seen as emulating the

U.S. agricultural experimental stations. These centers have high potential and, given time to get into full operation, should have a large influence on public education. They should give school administrators a knowledge base about educational practices that is as firm as that from which the county extension agent operates.

3. "Domestication" of Public Schools

To the list of factors which hinder change activities in public schools, a list which so far in my remarks includes the lack of a change agent and a weak knowledge base about innovations, let me add a third factor. This third factor has to do with organizational characteristics of schools and specifically with the relationship between the school as an organization and its clients.

When we talk about service organizations, those organizations which provide a self-improvement or rehabilitation function to clients which the organizations must motivate, it is clear that some of these organizations have the power or exercise the right to select its clients. Other service organizations, of which the school is one, cannot select their clients.

It is also obvious that clients are free to accept or reject the services provided by some service organizations but with some service organizations, the clients are *not* free to accept or reject the service—the clients of these organizations must accept the service. The school is one organization in the latter category.

Thus, some service organizations operate in an environment where they can select their clients and the clients are free to take or leave the service according to their desire. One of many examples of this type of organization is the *private college*. And some service organizations operate in an environment where they *cannot* select the clients they are to serve and the clients *must* accept the service. One of several examples of this type of organization is the *public school*.

The significance of the relationship with clients is implied in the label of "domesticated organization" which is given to organizations like the school which cannot select clients and where the client must accept the service. The label of domesticated organization is used to indicate that this class of organization is protected and cared for in a fashion similar to that of a domesticated animal. They are not compelled to attend to all of the ordinary and usual needs of an organization. For example, they do not compete with other organizations for clients; in fact, a steady flow of clients is assured. There is no struggle for survival for this type of organization—existence is guaranteed. Though this type of organization does compete in a restricted area for funds, funds are not closely tied to quality of performance. These organizations are domesticated in the sense that they are protected by the society they serve. The society sees the protection of these domesticated organizations as necessary to the maintenance of the social system and creates laws over and above those applying to organized action in general to care for these organizations.

The consequence of domesticating organizations, as far as organizational change is concerned, is to restrict the need for, and interest in, change because the environment of the domesticated organization in many important respects is more stable than it is in other types of organizations. When important elements of the environment are stable, as you know, the necessity for change is reduced.

Therefore, it seems reasonable to suggest that the domestication of public schools is a hinderance to change along with the lack of a change agent and a weak knowledge base about educational innovation.

THE IMPACT OF RESEARCH FINDINGS ON INNOVATION ADOPTION

Now let us return to the problems of the school superintendent as a change agent and ask the question of what guide lines are suggested for his action by educational research. What does research about the adoption of educational innovations tell the school administrator?

Research on the spread of educational innovations has several characteristics which set it apart from many other streams of diffusion research. One distinctive feature is that a vast amount of work has been done. It seems fair to say that the diffusion literature is as sophisticated and as well developed as any other area of scientific study to which educators have given their attention. Further, the study of the spread of educational practices bears the mark of one man. The late Paul Mort and his students seemed almost to have cornered the market on studies of the diffusion of educational innovations. This last feature has, however, apparently permitted a third and very important characteristic of such studies: an implicit asumption that characteristics of chief school officials are unimportant in explaining rates of adoption of innovations.

Mort and his students have displayed considerable ingenuity in the isolation of variables—usually relating to the economic base of the school district, ranging from expenditure per pupil to teachers' salaries—and in fitting the variables into accounting schemes.

A conclusion based on over 100 studies done in what I choose to call the Mort tradition is this—"If but one question can be asked, on the basis of which a prediction of rate of adoption of educational innovations is to be made, the question is: 'How much is spent per child?' " Said another way, school systems that are first to adopt educational innovation spend the most money per child and those last to adopt educational innovations spend the least amount per child.

Assuming some causes and effect relationship to be at work here, what does this finding, which comes out of a vast amount of research effort, suggest to the school superintendent? I believe that it suggests a clear line of action. If a school administrator wants his district to be on the so called leading edge in the development of public schools, his efforts above all else should be directed toward securing for his district as much money as possible and as few students as possible. I am sure this is well understood for we can all cite examples showing that this is exactly what some school districts attempt to do.

I think it is indeed fortunate, however, that this finding of the relationship between money spent per child and rates of adoption of educational innovations is being challenged by data which are now emerging.

In a recent study of the adoption of such educational practices as team teaching, modern math, foreign language instruction in the elementary grades, programmed instruction, ungraded primary classes, and accelerated programs in high schools among school systems in a county in western Pennsylvania, it was found that amount of money spent per child had a negative, insignificant correlation. That is, amount of money spent per child had no predictive power in relation to the rate of adoption of these innovations.

This is not a single finding in one county. The general finding was replicated in two ways. First, another research project was undertaken in the state of West Virginia and again it was found that the rate of adoption of these innovations was not significantly related to expenditure per child. And second, even though the expenditure level per child is considerably lower in West Virginia than it is in western Pennsylvania, there was found to be no material differences in the rates of adoptions of these innovations between these two regions of the country.

To my way of thinking, these rather recent findings which indicate no significant relationship between rate of adoption of educational innovations and expenditure per child, are indeed happy ones. They should be popular with school administrators because, for one thing, they break away from a mechanistic explanation and show the school administrator as something other than a victim of his local budget.

These findings coupled with others, which I will not bother to recite, for they are well covered in Everett Rogers' paper, give very clear evidence of the important role of school superintendents in the process of adopting educational innovations, and in general of the centrality of human rather than monetary aspects in the adoption process.

2

Planned Change
and
Organizational Health:
Figure and Ground

By
MATTHEW B. MILES

Planned Change and Organizational Health: Figure and Ground

Matthew B. Miles
Teachers College, Columbia University

ANY OBSERVER of the applied behavioral sciences today would have to note a remarkable interest in the entire problem of planned change. Scientists and practitioners alike are concerned with the stages of planned change in groups, organizations, and communities; with the question of how change processes can be managed in a meaningful sense of that word; and with the characteristics of the "change agent," that miraculous middleman between What Science Has Proved and What We Are Up Against. The very existence of this seminar is a case in point.

There is a growing literature, in journals as diverse as *Applied Anthropology* and *Petroleum Refiner;* there have already been thoughtful attempts to collect this literature, and to conceptualize the problems involved. (Lippitt, Watson and Westley, 1958; Bennis, Benne and Chinn, 1961). All this is gratifying to beleaguered school administrators—and to everyone who, following Kurt Lewin's most frequently-quoted dictum, believes that "there is nothing so practical as a good theory."

Yet it seems to me that there is an important, but often-overlooked aspect of what is being said and done about planned change: the notion that any particular planned change effort is deeply conditioned by the state of the system in which it takes place. For example, properties of the organization such as communication adequacy, and the distribution of influence have a powerful effect on the speed and durability of adoption of any particular innovation, from *English 2600* to data processing of teacher marks. To use an image from Gestalt psychology, specific planned change attempts have most typically been "in figure," occupying the focus of attention, while the organization itself has remained the "ground."

I believe this emphasis is both practically and theoretically unfortunate. It is time for us to recognize that successful efforts at planned change must take as a primary target the improvement of *organiza-*

tion health—the school system's ability not only to function effectively, but to develop and grow into a more fully-functioning system.

Perhaps I can illustrate my assertion that organization properties have often been treated peripherally, or left to sit as background phenomena. If you have examined the literature on the diffusion of innovations, perhaps with the aid of Everett Rogers' excellent compendium (1962) you will notice that a good deal of attention is paid to the individual innovator, to when he adopts the innovation, and why. But the literature remains nearly silent on the organizational setting in which innovation takes place. I suspect this has several antecedents.

For one thing, the typical adopter in most rural sociological studies is an individual farmer rather than a collectivity such as an organization. The farmer's role in the community setting turns out to be important, but aside from studies on "traditional" versus "modern" community norms, the influence of the larger social setting tends to be underplayed.

Paul Mort did, on the other hand, make extensive studies of innovation by organizations—school districts (see Ross, 1958). But Mort, far from being even an amateur sociologist, appeared almost aggressively ignorant of available knowledge about the functioning of organizations and communities. His "common sense" categories and demographic indices give us no inkling of what was really going on in the districts who supplied him with data.

Even Dick Carlson's (1964) study of the adoption of modern math by school superintendents suffers a bit, I think, from a kind of "great man" tendency; the internal dynamics of the school system are seen as less important than characteristics of the local superintendent, such as his position in the reference group of administrators in the region. His data are compelling, but I suspect they would have been even more powerful had he gone into more depth on the dynamics of the local setting.

From the anthropological side, I think it fair to say that there has been an over-emphasis on the properties of a particular innovation itself, its diffusion across systems, and its integration within systems —without a corresponding degree of interest in the dynamics and functioning of the receiving organization as such. Art Gallaher (1963) has thoughtfully discussed power structure in innovation-receiving systems, the actual prestige of advocates of the innovation, and other matters influencing how (or if) an innovation will be integrated into the local organization. But even here, I think the analysis is over-focused on the "thinginess" of the particular innovation, taking the local system itself as a kind of unmodifiable ground against which the innovation shows up in stark figure.

One more example. The currently wide-spread emphasis on the

importance of "dissemination of research findings," and even the recent effort of the U. S. Office to provide development and demonstration centers, likewise avoid the problem. They share the popular view that the *content* or demonstrated efficacy of a particular educational innovation, as such, is the crucial thing in determining whether or not it will be adopted and used effectively. As you can gather, I am taking a decidedly processual view here: organization dynamics are the focus of attention.

I hope I have not misrepresented the views of my colleagues. It would please me to be corrected, in fact. What I do want to counter in this paper is a set of assumptions (by scientists or practitioners) that organization properties—from decision-making methods to interpersonal climate—are simply "there," that they are relatively invariant, and cannot (or should not) themselves be made the subject of planned change efforts.

More generally, the position being taken is this. It seems likely that the state of health of an educational organization can tell us more than anything else about the probable success of any particular change effort. Economy of effort would suggest that we should look at the state of an organization's health as such, and try to improve it—in preference to struggling with a series of more or less inspired short-run change efforts as ends in themselves.

To analogize with persons for a minute: the neurotic who struggles through one unavailing search for "something new" after another will never be genuinely productive until he faces and works through fundamental problems of his own functioning. Genuine productiveness—in organizations as in persons—rests on a clear sense of identity, on adequate connection with reality, on a lively problem-solving stance, and on many other things, to which I would like to turn in a moment. Here I only wish to leave you with the root notion that attention to organization health ought to be priority one for any administrator seriously concerned with innovativeness in today's educational environment.

In the remainder of this paper, I should like, first, to deal with some problems in the very concept of health, both generally and as applied to organizations. The next section reviews the conception of "organization" employed in the rest of the paper, and outlines some dimensions of organization health as I see them. All this is rather general, and I should then like to turn to some discussion of the special properties of *educational* organizations, as such, and what their particular ways of departing from optimum organization health seem to be. Lastly, as an applied behavioral scientist, I would be remiss if I did not discuss some representative technologies for inducing organization health, and suggest some principles underlying them.

Most of this paper is frankly speculative, though it is informed by a good deal of current work in the applied behavioral sciences—and even, now and then, by some contact with phenomena such as super-intendents, principals, teachers and children. All of the notions in the paper need vigorous discussion and testing.

Some Problems in the Concept of "Health"

The historical, common-sense notion of health is that it represents absence of illness, disease, suffering, wrongness in an organism. If not arrested, a serious "sickness" may lead to irreversible changes, such as organ impairment, atrophy or death. But beginning (to my knowledge) with the interesting British work in preventive medicine dubbed the "Peckham Experiment," there has been more and more medical concern with the notion of positive well-being or optimal functioning. That is, disease-freeness, in and of itself, does not guar-antee that an organism will in fact be coping with life's adventures with a sense of *élan*, and growing while it does so.

This conception of positive health—in many ways a sneaky, vague notion—has also been receiving more and more attention in the mental health literature (see Jahoda, 1958). And there is increasing interest in the fields of psychotherapy and human relations training with the notion of "self-actualization." Both "positive health" and "self-actualization" imply a considerable gap between sheer disease-free-ness, and something that might be called the fully functioning human being. This is an attractive idea; it is consistent with much of our common sense experience, and it caters to the American notion of the (nearly) infinitely-improvable man.

But even if something like "positive health" or "self-actualization" can be said to exist—and Maslow's (1950) case studies are instructive and plausible in this respect—there are some traps and difficulties in applying such concepts to organization functioning. One, of course, is the tendency to go "over-organismic," reifying the organization into some kind of gigantic person, or least organism. This, of course, leads into the hoary disputation about whether systems larger than that of the individual person are "real" (see, for example, Warriner, 1956), a totally unprofitable byway which I do not propose to enter at the moment.

Another danger is that the notion of health implies "sickness"; school administrators are having enough difficulty as it is without being accused of being at the helm of pathological vessels on the stormy seas of innovation. The very image of "sickness" itself diverts attention away from the notion of positive growth and development, implying that only correction of some negative or painful state is required.

Finally, there are the risks involved in any discussion involv-ing "ideal types"—distortion of reality, or blindness to large portions of it, and a prevalence of normative, preachment-type statement-making about any particular organization (or, more usually, *all* organizations).

All these objections have some validity; I do not propose to eradicate them here, only to bring them to awareness, so they do not hamper the subsequent discussion unduly. In brief, the intellectual risks of an "organization health" approach seem to me far outweighed by the advantages. A reasonably clear conception of organization health would seem to be an important prerequisite to a wide range of activities involving organizations: research of any meaningful sort; attempts to improve the organization as a place to live, work, and learn; and—not least—the day-to-day operations of any particular organization, such as your own school system.[1]

ORGANIZATIONS: THEIR NATURE

Formal definitions show that the author of the paper has paid his debt to "the literature"; they may sometimes even help in de-limiting the sphere of discussion. "Organization" is here treated as a special case of the more general concept "system," more particularly "open system." The latter is defined as:

A bounded collection of interdependent parts, devoted to the accomplishment of some goal or goals, with the parts maintained in a steady state in relation to each other and the environment by means of (1) standard modes of operation, and (2) feedback from the environment about the consequences of system actions. (Miles, 1964 a, p. 13)

Argyris (1964, p. 120) poses a broadly similar definition: "(1) a plurality of parts, [which] (2) maintaining themselves through their interrelatedness and, (3) achieving specific objective(s), (4) while accomplishing (2) and (3) adapt to the external environment thereby (5) maintaining their interrelated state of parts."

Either of these definitions would apply to a system such as a candle flame, an air-conditioning unit, or a school district. For our purposes, it is perhaps sufficient to say that the above definitions, in the special case of the "organization," are expected to apply to social systems larger than a face-to-face group, and with a reasonable degree of goal specification (this latter to exclude larger systems, such as communities and nations).

Somewhat more specifically, reference to Figure 1 will indicate the notion "educational organization" used as a backdrop for this paper. Notice that the usual hierarchical arrangement is absent, since the "parts" are not seen as persons or work groups, but as social-psychological components of the system which cross-cut persons and groups.

---

[1] For additional comments on the importance of the concept of organization health, see Bennis (1962).

The figure indicates that the organization exists in an environment from which it receives inputs (money, personnel, and children) and to which it releases outputs in terms of goal achievement, and morale and learning motivation of the clients in the organization (children).

Figure 1

SCHEMATIC MODEL OF ORGANIZATION FUNCTIONING AND CHANGE ENVIRONMENT

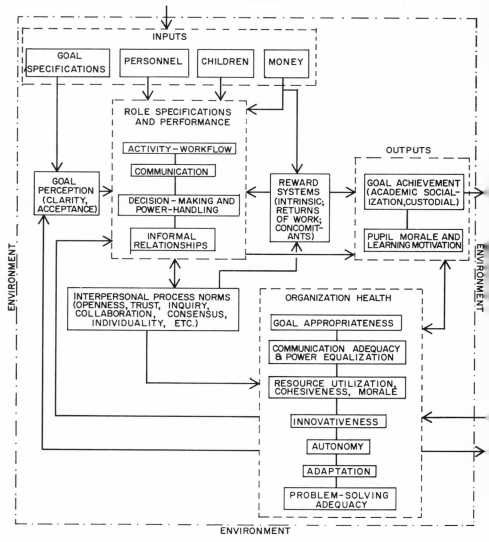

Between the input and the output, to paraphrase T. S. Eliot, falls the shadow of a number of other components. The inhabitants of an educational organization must have reasonably clear perceptions of the goal or goals to which the system is devoted; these in turn affect role specifications and performance for the inhabitants. Systems of reward and penalty regulate role performance, as do the norms governing the style of interpersonal transactions in the system. The arrows in the diagram are intended to indicate directions of influence between parts of the system, as well as to suggest that a variety of feedback loops exist which serve to maintain the system in a reasonably steady state.

If all goes well, desired system outputs are achieved. But this is not all: above and beyond the network of parts and their functioning, we can conceive of a set of system "health" characteristics, which have to do with the continued adequacy and viability of the organization's coping. More of this below. Here it is perhaps sufficient to sketch out the schematic model, and point out that it assumes nothing about the specific kinds of structures—planful or emergent—appearing in any particular system. The model will presumably fit a classical pyramidal scheme, as well as a number of more or less radical variants from this (e.g., those suggested by Argyris, 1964).

Organization Health

Our present thinking about organization health is that it can be seen as a set of fairly durable *second-order* system properties, which tend to transcend short-run effectiveness. A healthy organization in this sense not only survives in its environment, but continues to cope adequately over the long haul, and continuously develops and extends its surviving and coping abilities. Short-run operations on any particular day may be effective or ineffective, but continued survival, adequate coping, and growth are taking place.

A *steadily* ineffective organization would presumably not be heatlhy; on balance, "health" implies a summation of effective short-run coping. But notice that an organization *may* cope effectively in the short run (as for example by a speed-up or a harsh cost-cutting drive), but at the cost of longer-run variables, such as those noted below. The classic example, of course, is an efficiency drive which cuts short-run costs and results in long-run labor dissatisfaction and high turnover.

To illustrate in more detail what is meant by "second-order property," here is a list of ten dimensions of organization health that seem plausible to me. Many of them are drawn by heuristic analogy from the behavior of persons or small groups; this does *not* mean, of course, that organizations necessarily are precisely homologous to persons or groups—only that thinking in this way may get us somewhere on what, it must be admitted, is a very complex problem indeed. Here then are ten dimensions. They are not, of course mutually exclusive, and interact with each other vigorously within any particular organization. Both Jahoda (1958) and Argyris (1964) have commented on the importance of a multiple-criterion approach to the assessment of health, given the present state of our knowledge and the fact, that as a college roommate of mine once remarked with blinding insight, "You know, everything is really connected to everything else."

The first three dimensions are relatively "tasky," in that they deal with organizational goals, the transmission of messages, and the way in which decisions are made.

1. *Goal focus.* In a healthy organization, the goal (or more usually goals) of the system would be reasonably clear to the system members, and reasonably well accepted by them.[2] This clarity and acceptance, however, should be seen as a necessary but insufficient condition for organization health. The goals must also be *achievable* with existing or available resources, and be *appropriate*—more or less congruent with the demands of the environment. The last feature may be most critical. Switching back to the person level for a moment, consider the obsessive patient who sets the clear, accepted, achievable goal for himself of washing his hands 250 times a day. The question remains: is this an appropriate goal in light of what else there is to do in life?

2. *Communication adequacy.* Since organizations are not simultaneous face-to-face systems like small groups, the movement of information within them becomes crucial. This dimension of organization health implies that there is relatively distortion-free communication "vertically," "horizontally," and across the boundary of the system to and from the surrounding environment. That is, information travels reasonably well—just as the healthy person "knows himself" with a minimum level of repression, distortion, etc. In the healthy organization, there is good and prompt sensing of internal strains; there are enough data about problems of the system to insure that a good diagnosis of system difficulties can be made. People have the information they need, and have gotten it without exerting undue efforts, such as those involved in moseying up to the superintendent's secretary, reading the local newspaper, or calling excessive numbers of special meetings.

---

[2] Note that the question of actual goal achievement as such is here conceived of as separate, analytically speaking, from the question of organization health. Argyris has suggested that organization effectiveness, a concept resembling the health notion, resides in the organization's ability to (1) achieve goals, (2) maintain itself internally, (3) engage in adaptation processes with the environment— and to accomplish these three "core activities" at a constant or increasing level of effectiveness, given the same or decreasing increments in energy input (Argyris, 1964, p. 123). This three-way scheme is also used in the present discussion.

3. *Optimal power equalization.* In a healthy organization the distribution of influence is relatively equitable. Subordinates (if there is a formal authority chart) can influence upward, and even more important—as Likert (1961) has demonstrated—they perceive that their boss can do likewise with *his* boss. In such an organization, inter-group struggles for power would not be bitter, though inter-group conflict, (as in every human system known to man) would undoubtedly be present. The basic stance of persons in such an organization, as they look up, sideways and down, is that of collaboration rather than explicit or implicit coercion. The units of the organization (persons in roles, work groups, etc.) would stand in an interdependent relationship to each other, with rather less emphasis on the ability of a "master" part to control the entire operation. The exertion of influence in a healthy organization would presumably rest on the competence of the influencer *vis-à-vis* the issue at hand, his stake in the outcome, and the amount of knowledge or data he has—rather than on his organizational position, personal charisma, or other factors with little direct relevance to the problem at hand.

These then are three "task-centered" dimensions of organization health. A second group of three dimensions deals essentially with the internal state of the system, and its inhabitants' "maintenance" needs. These are resource utilization, cohesiveness, and morale.

4. *Resource utilization.* We say of a healthy person, such as a second-grader, that he is "working up to his potential." To put this another way, the classroom system is evoking a contribution from him at an appropriate and goal-directed level of tension. At the organization level, "health" would imply that the system's inputs, particularly the personnel, are used effectively. The overall coordination is such that people are neither overloaded nor idling. There is a minimal sense of strain, generally speaking (in the sense that trying to do something with a weak or inappropriate structure puts strain on that structure). In the healthy organization, people may be working very hard indeed, but they feel that they are not working against themselves, or against the organization. The fit between people's own dispositions and the role demands of the system is good. Beyond this, people feel reasonably "self-actualized"; they not only "feel good" in their jobs, but they have a genuine sense of learning, growing, and developing as persons in the process of making their organizational contribution.

5. *Cohesiveness.* We think of a healthy person as one who has a clear sense of identity; he knows who he is, underneath all the specific goals he sets for himself. Beyond this, he *likes himself*; his stance toward life does not require self-derogation, even when there are aspects of his behavior which are unlovely or ineffective. By analogy

at the organization level, system health would imply that the organization knows "who it is." Its members feel attracted to membership in the organization. They want to stay with it, be influenced by it, and exert their own influence in the collaborative style suggested above.

6. *Morale*. The history of this concept in the social-psychological literature is so appalling that I hesitate to introduce it at all. The implied notion is one of well-being or satisfaction. Satisfaction is not enough for health, of course; a person may report feelings of well-being and satisfaction in his life, while successfully denying deeplying hostilities, anxieties, and conflicts. Yet it still seems useful to evoke, at the organization level, the idea of morale: a summated set of individual sentiments, centering around feelings of well-being, satisfaction, and pleasure, as opposed to feelings of discomfort, unwished-for strain and dissastisfaction. In an *un*healthy system, life might be perceived rosily as "good," or as unabashedly bad; in a healthy organization it is hard to entertain the idea that the dominant personal response of organization members would be anything else than one of well-being.

Finally, there are four more dimensions of organization health, which deal with growth and changefulness: the notions of innovativeness, autonomy, adaptation *vis-à-vis* the environment, and problem-solving adequacy.

7. *Innovativeness*. A healthy system would tend to invent new procedures, move toward new goals, produce new kinds of products, diversify itself, and become more rather than less differentiated over time. In a sense, such a system could be said to grow, develop, and change, rather than remaining routinized, and standard. The analogue here is to the self-renewing properties of a Picasso; or to Schachtel's (1959) "activity" orientation (curious, exploring) as contrasted with "embeddedness" orientation (tension-reducing, protective) in persons.[3]

8. *Autonomy*. The healthy person acts "from his own center outward." Seen in a training or therapy group, for example, such a person appears nearly free of the need to submit dependently to authority figures, *and* from the need to rebel and destroy symbolic fathers of any kind. A healthy organization, similarly, would not respond passively to demands from the outside, feeling itself the tool of the environment, and it would not respond destructively or rebelliously

---

[3] Clark (1962) has suggested that organization health resides primarily in the continuous possibility of *both* kinds of orientation: toward change and development, and for stability and maintenance. This dual possibility should be realized, he suggests, at the personal, group, inter-group, and total organizational levels.

to perceived demands either. It would tend to have a kind of independence from the environment, in the same sense that the healthy person, while he has transactions with others, does not treat their responses as *determinative* of his own behavior.

9. *Adaptation.* The notions of autonomy and innovativeness are both connected with the idea that a healthy person, group, or organization is in realistic, effective contact with the surroundings. When environmental demands and organization resources do not match, a problem-solving, re-structuring approach evolves in which *both* the environment and the organization become different in some respect. More adequate, continued coping of the organization, as a result of changes in the local system, the relevant portions of the environment, or more usually both, occurs. And such a system has sufficient stability and stress tolerance to manage the difficulties which occur during the adaptation process. Perhaps inherent in this notion is that the system's ability to bring about corrective change in itself is faster than the change cycle in the surrounding environment. Explanations for the disappearance of dinosaurs vary, but it is quite clear that in some way this criterion was not met.

10. *Problem-solving adequacy.* Finally, any healthy organism— even one as theoretically impervious to fallibility as a computer— *always* has problems, strains, difficulties, and instances of ineffective coping. The issue is not the presence or absence of problems, therefore, but the *manner* in which the person, group, or organization copes with problems. Argyris (1964) has suggested that in an effective system, problems are solved with minimal energy; they stay solved; and the problem-solving mechanisms used are not weakened, but maintained or strengthened. An adequate organization, then, has well-developed structures and procedures for sensing the existence of problems, for inventing possible solutions, for deciding on the solutions, for implementing them, and for evaluating their effectiveness. Such an organization would conceive of its own operations (whether directed outward to goal achievement, inward to maintenance, or inward-outward to problems of adaptation) as being *controllable.* We would see active coping with problems, rather than passive withdrawing, compulsive responses, scapegoating, or denial.

Here then are ten dimensions of a healthy organization,[4] stated abstractly, even vaguely in many instances. They must, of course, be

---

[4] Little has been said here about the actual form of the organization which is most likely to meet these criteria of organizational health at some optimal level. Some applied work in organization change (Argyris, 1964; Bennis, 1962) suggests that strongly pyramidal organizations designed around strict division of labor, accountability, limited span of control, etc., are uniquely *ill*-fitted to the demands of survival in today's world. Argyris (1964) has suggested a number of alternatives to the pyramidal model, (such as the use of temporary "product teams" with

operationalized into meaningful indicators of organization functioning; the staff of our project is currently into this with more than a little trepidation, but with keen interest to see whether these ways of viewing the health of a system prove to have a reasonable amount of empirical steam behind them.

THE SPECIAL CASE OF EDUCATIONAL ORGANIZATIONS

These dimensions can presumably be applied to any type of organization. Much of the theory and empirical data on which they are based was generated in industrial organizations in which "organization improvement" programs have become more and more widespread in the last few years. (See, for example, Bennis, 1963, 1964.) We need, however, to determine the special properties of *educational* systems (if any) which pre-dispose them to particular types of ill health. It is also necessary to examine whether the technologies of organization improvement which have proved successful industrially need adaption in certain directions before they are likely to be efficacious in schools. If this is not done, we might well expect a recrudescence of the unfortunate enthusiasm of schoolmen for Taylorism and "scientific management" which occurred in the first decades of this century. (See the excellent treatment of this appalling subject in Callahan & Button, 1964.)

In our own time, it has taken a good deal of agitation by people like Dan Griffiths to get school administrators and professors of education to accept the possibility that the school is in fact an organization, and as such shares certain properties with all other organizations, and that administrative theory, if well developed in any field of human endeavor, could apply to the school business. This is quite correct. However, emphasis on the commonality of all types of organizations has tended to obscure the fact that educational systems have special properties which condition the propositions of organization theory in reasonably predictable ways. What, then, are some of these properties?

1. *Goal ambiguity.* For many different reasons, it has seemed difficult to specify the output of educational organizations very precisely. Some of this is realistic: change in human beings is going on, with presumably cumulative effects over a long period of time. But part of this output measurement difficulty also seems to be a form of organiza-

---

power base on functional contribution rather than position) which he feels are not only more likely to lead in the direction of organization health but respect the "essential properties" of organizations as open systems. Empirical data on this question are not numerous; however, work with communication nets in small simulated organizations has suggested that relatively loose, power-equalized, full-communication models of organization are much more effective than traditional models when the environment is shifting and changing. This finding also appeared in a study of Scottish electronic firms by Burns and Stalker (1961). See also Likert (1961).

tion defense or protection against criticism from the surrounding environment (see below).

Whatever the reasons, supposed "unmeasurability" of organizational output (hence, of the effectiveness of particular role occupants) seems a fairly durable feature of educational organizations as we know them today.

In addition, certain goals of the school (such as "academic learning") are often given primacy in public pronouncements while others (for example, the socialization of achievement motivation and appropriate *Gesellschaftlich* behavior for the incoming denizens of an industrial society) are treated as background phenomena. Still others (such as keeping the kids off the streets and out of Mother's way—call it custodial care) are usually taboo as legitimate goal statements.[5]

It is possible, of course, that school system goals are not all that unmeasurable and ambiguous. In some exploratory interviewing we have been doing in two suburban school systems, teachers and principals, almost without exception, denied that "it is difficult to know when you are doing a good job"[6] and denied that "disagreement over the goals of the school" was present. We intend to pursue this further, because our hunch is that such protestations of agreement reflect defensive solutions to the actual problems of goal ambiguity and goal disagreement, which do in fact exist.

I believe that this ambiguity and pseudo-consensus around school output measurement encourages the institutionalization and ossification of teaching procedures. If it cannot really be determined whether one course of action leads to more output than another, then why stop lecturing? There is a further consequence (stemming particularly from the unacknowledged but powerful custodial function of the school): highly rigid time and personnel allocations in most American schools. Hall passes, the forty-seven-minute period, and the difficulty some teachers have in finding time to go to the toilet are all examples. It is interesting that the increasing use of computers for class scheduling has not, to my knowledge, exploited the enormous potential of information-processing machines for making a *more* rather than less flexible learning environment. In any event, I wish only to make the point that goal ambiguity and procedural rigidity may very well turn out to be closely connected.

2. *Input variability.* Another, possibly unique, property of educational organizations is a very wide variation in input from the environ-

---

[5] If you doubt for a minute that custodial care is an important goal of the American public school, try this "Gedanken-experiment." Which would be the most effective form of teacher strike: (a) for teachers to stay home; (b) for teachers to come to school, but teach the children nothing?

[6] This is a remarkable assertion, in light of the encyclopedic (and to me gloomily inconclusive) research findings on teacher effectiveness (see Gage, 1963b).

ment, particularly in relation to children and personnel. Since the school is defined in America as publicly responsible, it must accept children of a very wide range of ability and motivation to carry out its activities (this holds true, of course, for custodial and socialization goals as well as academic learning goals). The current stress on programs for the "culturally deprived" only serves to divert attention from the fact that the American schools seem never to have been able to cope effectively with children from lower socioeconomic levels.[7]

'This is no place to review in any detail the problem of variability in teacher performance, but here again it is important to note that the range of intellectual ability, interpersonal skill and knowledge of subject matter among teachers is probably at least as great as that among pupils. This variability causes considerable stress in educational organizations, and develops the need to provide teaching personnel with methods and procedures which are (in effect) teacher-proof. Wayland (1964) has reviewed this problem as a function of the enormous historical expansion of the scope of American education; he suggests that the teacher's role is now essentially that of a bureaucratic functionary, all protestations of "professionalism" to the contrary.

3. *Role performance invisibility.* Classrooms are in effect the production departments of the educational enterprise; in them teachers teach. Yet, this role performance is relatively invisible to status equals or superiors. Children can observe, usually very acutely, the quality of a teacher's execution of her role, but they are not allowed to comment on this, and have few (if any) sanctions to bring to bear. Thus, rewards in the teaching profession seem relatively detached from others' estimates of one's performance; the average teacher, as Lortie (1961) has pointed out, gains most satisfaction from intrinsic properties of the role behavior involved. Teaching thus becomes a craft-like occupation, rather than a profession, and substitute criteria for teaching effectiveness, such as "how interested the kids are" begin to appear and are used vigorously. Perhaps this is what our teachers meant when they said it was not difficult to know when they were doing a good job.

4. *Low interdependence.* A further characteristic of educational organizations, when compared with thing-producing systems, seems to be a relatively low interdependence of parts. Teacher A's failure to teach anything to her minions affects the job-relevant behavior of teacher B very little—except in a rather diffuse, blaming sense, as when junior high-school teachers devoutly declare their belief that basic skills are not present in newly-arrived seventh graders.

This low interdependence has several consequences. First, it tends to reinforce the pyramidal "man-to-man" style of supervision which

---

[7] See, for example, the really staggering data on reading retardation and advancement as a function of social class in Barton and Wilder (1964).

Likert (1961) and others have shown to be inimical to organization effectiveness. In the case of teachers of young children, it tends to promote a kind of infantilism and boredom; in many teachers, as suggested by a recent study (Peterson, 1964) the peak of productive contribution tends to be in the twenties, with distancing from students and potential routinization starting in the mid-thirties. The reported stresses and strains in most accounts of team teaching—an attempt to increase interdependence in educational organizations—are mute testimony to the strength with which "separatist" norms have become institutionalized in the American public school.[8]

High interdependence is not without its difficulties, of course. As Golembiewski (1964) has pointed out, the classical division of industrial organizations into specialized departments tends to promote hostility, competitiveness, and disjunction between the authority system and other aspects of the organiaztion such as communication patterns, friendship relationships, and work flow. He suggests an alternative organization model involving the existence of "product divisions," each of which contains in it all the specialties necessary to undertake an operation such as buying materials for, producing and marketing a washing machine. Schools are organized in a product division manner, in effect. But Golembiewski's analysis—this is crucial—depends on the existence of simple, rapidly-available output measures, so that the performance of a product division can be monitored. As we have seen, the absence of such measures—and more fundamentally, the belief that they can never be produced—is a serious barrier to the effectiveness of educational organizations.

5. *Vulnerability*. The American public school, even more than other public organizations, is subject to control, criticism, and a wide variety of "legitimate" demands from the surrounding environment: everyone is a stockholder. Any public organization tends to generate this type of relationship with systems and persons outside its boundary. But a people-processing organization such as the school is dealing with extremely valuable property—children—who return to their parents each night with more or less accurate news of how they have been treated. Thus, in the special kind of organization termed a school, almost any role occupant—board member, superintendent, principal, staff specialist, or teacher can be criticized by parents or citizens at large. To the system inhabitants, the organization skin seems extremely thin. Many kinds of ingenious defenses are adopted to solve this

---

[8] Lortie's (1961) comments on a three-part norm system are relevant here: He comments on the teacher as subscribing to the following beliefs: a) the teacher should be free of interference in his teaching; b) other teachers should be considered and treated as equals (in spite of the fact that they obviously differ in interests and skill); c) teachers should act in a friendly manner toward one another in informal contacts. Note that these norms reinforce each other in such a way as to inhibit effective, interdependent work.

problem—policies about visiting the classroom, brain-washing of new board members by the superintendent and the old members (cf. Sieber, in press), buffer devices such as the PTA, and so on. Yet, the fact remains that a consumer who doesn't like the octane rating of his gasoline cannot go to the refinery and criticize the operation of a cat-cracker—but a parent who feels conflicted about her child's reading ability can be pretty violent with the first grade teacher. (I might comment that this vulnerability seems most sharp when viewed from the inside. Many parents apparently feel that the school is impregnable, and that they must not raise complaints, rock the boat, etc.)

In any event, this state of affairs represents, I believe, a serious failure of adaptation skills of schools as organizations, and tends to reduce school system autonomy sharply. In recent years, I have met only one school superintendent who told me he was going ahead actively (and successfully) with curriculum and organization changes to which a majority of his community were opposed. As it turned out, he was an old private school man.

6. *Lay-professional control problems.* Public schools are governed by laymen, most of whom have not been inside a school for twenty years prior to their succession to the board. As a result, they often agree tacitly or explicitly on a division of labor with the superintendent and his staff (the policy—procedure distinction developed by Brickell and Davies is one such example). But even where the board is "well trained" and leaves the execution of policy to the superintendent, notice that the question of *educational policy* determination still remains a moot one.

And there are internal lay-professional problems as well. In many respects, the principal of an elementary or high school, in terms of expert knowledge, may find himself far behind the capabilities of particular teachers on his staff—and is in this sense a layman as well. The problems of organizations with high proportions of professionals have been studied vigorously (ex: hospitals, and research organizations); I only wish to indicate here that the fruits of such study so far have found little application in schools.[9]

7. *Low technological investment.* Lastly, it seems very clear that the amount of technology per worker in schools is relatively low. From 60% to 75% of a local school system's budget ordinarily goes to salary, with a fraction for equipment and materials. Even if we count buildings as "technological investment," the picture is rather different from that in most industries. This has consequences: social transac-

---

[9] It is interesting to note that the greatest inroads of applied behavioral science seem to have been in research-based organizations, in areas such as aerospace, electronics, and petroleum refining. Why this has not happened in schools (and universities!) is an interesting question. It may very well be that a knowledge-*spreading* organization (such as a school) operates rather differently from a knowledge-*making* one (such as a research group).

tions, rather than socio-technical transactions, come to be the major mode of organization production. Because of this, it is possible that education, as James Finn has suggested, has never made it out of the folk culture stage. And we are back once again to goal ambiguity and its problems.

These, then, strike me as special strains, ways in educational organizations as such and the public school in particular depart from the generalized model of organization health outlined earlier. In sum, I would suggest that, in terms of the dimensions above, the major difficulties to be expected in most public schools would center around goal focus, (as a consequence of goal ambiguity), difficulties in communication adequacy and power equalization stemming from low interdependence; and perhaps most centrally, failures in innovativeness, autonomy, adaptation, and problem-solving adequacy, because of vulnerability and lay-professional conflict.

Interestingly enough, I do not see any clear reason for believing that internal "maintenance problems" (such as those involved in effective resource utilization, cohesiveness, and morale) are sharp points of strain in most school systems; it may very well be that low interdependence, plus orientation to a professional reference group, carry with them a willingness to "settle for less' than the optimum in these areas.

THE INDUCTION OF ORGANIZATION HEALTH

The particular degree of health of any local school system, given a multiple-criterion approach such as that suggested here, undoubtedly varies from time to time. A question of considerable interest is: what can be done to induce a greater degree of organization health in any particular system? By now a fair amount of experience exists, drawn from the interesting blend of consultation and research in which an increasing number of behavioral scientists now find themselves involved, primarily with industrial organizations. These methods can perhaps most usefully be considered as *interventions* in the on-going life of a system; this term implies an action which interferes with or reorients processes—either pathological or normal—ordinarily occurring in the system. A teacher's intervention in a child's problem-solving serves to reorient his thinking; perhaps more importantly, it can aid the child to mobilize his own energies more effectively. Thus the usual aim of an intervention is to start internal change processes going in the system at hand, rather than only causing an immediate change.

Below are described six interventions aimed at improving organization health.[10] In some cases, plausible statements can be made about

---

[10] See Bennis (1963, 1964) for a thorough review of alternative approaches being used.

which dimensions of health are most typically influenced by a particular intervention. For the most part, however, we do not really know; it is exactly the function of our research project to discover how these are likely to work in educational organizations. In conclusion, some common principles underlying the six interventions are discussed.

1. *Team training.* In this approach, the members of an intact work group (for example, the superintendent and his central office personnel) meet for a period of several days away from their offices, with consultant help. They examine their own effectiveness as a problem solving team, the role of each member in the group and how it affects the group and the person himself, and the operations of the group in relation to its organizational environment. This problem-solving may be based on fairly careful prior data collection from individuals as to their views on the current problems of the system; these data are summarized and form the beginning of the group's agenda. Occasionally, exercises and theoretical material on group and organization functioning may be supplied by the outside consultant.

Under these circumstances, the members of the group usually improve in their abilities to express feelings directly, and to listen to—and understand—each other. Communication adequacy is thus considerably increased. The members also deal with internal conflicts in the team, and learn to solve problems more effectively as a unit, thus presumably increasing their ability to meet the demands placed upon them by other parts of the system. Over a period of time, beginning with the top decision-making group of the system, this intervention may be repeated with other groups as well. Industrial programs of this sort have been described by Argyris (1962) and Blake and Mouton (1962).

2. *Survey feedback.* In this approach, data bearing on attitudes, opinions, and beliefs of members of a system are collected via questionnaire. An external researcher summarizes the data for the organization as a whole, and for each of a number of relevant work groups. Each work group, under the guidance of its own superior, and perhaps with consultant help, examines its own summarized data, in comparison with those for the organization as a whole. The group makes plans for change stemming from these discussions and carries them out. The focus of this intervention is on many or all of the work groups within a total setting. The aim is to free up communication, leading to goal clarification and problem-solving work. The relative objectification involved in looking at data helps to reduce feelings of being misunderstood and isolated, and makes problems more susceptible to solution, rather than retaining them as a focus for blaming, scapegoating, griping and so on. For an account of survey feedback procedure, see Mann (1961); Gage (1963a) has tried a similar ap-

proach effectively with student-to-teacher feedback, and is now studying teacher-to-principal feedback.

3. *Role workshop*. Sometimes called the "horizontal slice" meeting, this intervention involves all the people in a particular role (for example, elementary principal). They fill out research instruments dealing with role expectations which various others hold for them, the fit between their own wishes and these expectations, their actual role performance, etc. These data are summarized, and form the vehicle for a series of activities (discussion, role practice, decision-making exercises, problem-solving and so on) at a workshop attended by all the people in the role. The main focus here is on role clarity, effectiveness, and improved fit between the person and the role. By sharing common role problems, people occupying the role may develop alternative solutions which result in better performance of that role and more "self-actualized" operation in general.

4. *"Target setting" and supporting activities*. In this approach, periodic meetings are held between a superior and each of his subordinates, separately. In a school system, this might involve the superintendent and his staff members, or a principal and his teachers. The work of each subordinate is reviewed in relation to organizational and personal goals, and the superior and subordinate agree collaboratively on new targets for the subordinate's work and personal development. These "targets" are in turn reviewed after some work time (usually six months or so) has elapsed. During that period, other activities such as role meetings, consultation, self-operated data collection, academic courses, and workshops, may be engaged in by the subordinate to develop needed skills and understandings as he works toward the collaboratively-set goals. The focus of attention here is the working relationship between superior and subordinate, and the degree to which they are together able to help the subordinate grow and develop on the job. Improved trust, feelings of support, better and more satisfying role performance, and more open communication usually result. Zander (1963) has reviewed thoroughly the problems and values of performance appraisal, including commentary on the target-setting approach.

5. *Organizational diagnosis and problem-solving*. This intervention involves a residential meeting of members of an intact work group, usually at the top of the organization (or in small organizations, up to size 40-50, the entire work force). They meet for several days to identify problems facing the system, and the reasons for the existence of these; to invent possible solutions; to decide on needed system changes; and to plan implementation of these through regular channels and newly-constructed ones. It differs from team training as described above in that relatively less attention is given to team relation-

ships and interpersonal effectiveness as such, and more to system problems in the large. The main focus of attention is on the organization and its current functioning. The improvement of problem-solving activity and communication adequacy are typical results. For an account of two such meetings conducted with an industrial organization, see Zand, Miles, and Lytle (forthcoming).

6. *Organizational experiment.* In this approach, a major organizational variable of interest is changed *directly*,[11] by agreement of the responsible administrators, and needed implementation efforts. One such approach is described vividly by Morse and Reimer (1956): in several divisions of a large organization, the level of decision-making was moved radically downward, thus giving more autonomy to subordinates; in several other divisions the level of decision-making was moved up; and in several divisions no change was made. Such an approach requires the careful collection of pre-post data, and the use of control groups in order to test the consequences of the change. The halo of "experiment" is an aid to acceptance, since the arrangement is seen as not only temporary, but scientific, and responsibly managed. Such an approach ordinarily includes a feedback stage, in which the results are examined carefully and implications for the continuing functioning of the organization drawn.

These, then, are six possible approaches to the induction of organization health. Certain common threads appear to flow through all of them.

1. *Self-study.* These approaches reject the "technocratic" change model involving the recommendations of a detached expert, and actively involve the system itself in what might be called organizational introspection. The same holds true for approaches involving group self-study for various teams in the organization, and personal introspection and re-examination by role occupants.

In common with the action research movement in education, these approaches also carry the assumption that an operant stance on the part of the organization is both theoretically and practically preferable to the problems involved in dependence on outsiders for system change.

2. *Relational emphasis.* These approaches do not conceive of the organization as a collection of jobs with isolated persons in them, but as a network of groups and role relationships; it is the functioning of these groups and relationships, as such, which requires examination and self-operated, experimental alteration. The aim is not to ferret

---

[11] I am reminded of Hollis Caswell's classic remark when asked in 1943 how the newly-formed Horace Mann-Lincoln Institute would proceed in its program of school experimentation: "We'll change the curriculum by changing it."

out and change the "attitude" of old-fogey Principal A, but to focus on the relationships and group settings in which Principal A's attitudes are evoked.

3. *Increased data flow.* These approaches all involve the heightening or intensification of communication, especially vertically, but also diagonally and horizontally. New feedback loops are often built in to the existing system. The use of status-equalizing devices such as intensive residential meetings also encourages fuller and freer flow of information through channels which may have been blocked or have always carried distorted messages.

4. *Norms as a change target.* By focusing on groups and relationships, and increasing data flow, these approaches have the effect of altering existing norms which regulate interpersonal transactions in the organization. If, for example, a work group where the norms are "play it close to the vest, and don't disagree with the boss" engages in a team training session, it is quite likely—since all group members have participated in the experience—that norms such as "be open about your feelings whether or not they tally with the boss' wishes" will develop. These approaches thus have a strong culture-changing component, based on intensive, data-based interaction with others.[12]

5. *Temporary-system approach.* But norm-changing is by definition very difficult under the usual pressures of day-to-day operation in the organization. "Business as usual" has to prevail. Most of the interventions described involve the use of residential meetings, which constitute a detached, "cultural island" approach to organizational introspection and self-correction. They are in effect temporary systems,[13] where new norms can develop, and where, given the suspension of the usual pressures, meaningful changes can be made in the structure and functioning of the permanent system.

6. *Expert facilitation.* All of these interventions also include the presence of a semi-detached consultant figure, whose main functions are to facilitate, provoke, and support the efforts of the system to understand itself, free up communication and engage in more adequate problem-solving behavior. The outsider role, however, is seen as impermanent; it is only associated with the system during the actual period of the intervention itself. If the intervention is successful, the

---

12 In retrospect, the crucial role of norms in the maintenance of organizational health has probably been underplayed in this paper. In our research, we are planning to collect data on norms such as those regulating interpersonal authenticity and awareness, trust, objectivity, collaboration, altruistic concern, consensual decision-making, innovativeness, and creativity. Most of these are directly co-ordinated to the dimensions of organizational health reviewed above.

13 See Miles (1964) for an analysis of the special properties of temporary systems for change-inducing purposes.

organization itself continues the self-corrective processes which have been begun by the intervention.

Whether or not these interventions, drawn from work with thing-producing organizations, can be used plausibly with people-processing organizations such as schools is an interesting question, to which my colleagues and I are beginning to gather some answers. Our impulse at the moment is to believe that the answer will be affirmative. With the assistance of two or three school systems, we expect to have some empirical data on intervention results in about two years, an eventuality to which we look forward with a good deal of pleasure.

In Conclusion

It might be useful to point out in conclusion that the position taken in this paper is *not* that an organization must necessarily be brought to a state of perfect health before it can engage in any meaningful short-run innovative projects at all. Rather, we feel it is quite likely that the very act of carrying out small scale projects in planned change can undoubtedly strengthen the health of an educational organization—but only if *direct attention is paid concurrently to the state of the organization.* The basic innovative project, we believe, must be one of organization development itself.

This paper comes out of preliminary work in the Project on Organization Development in Schools, at the Horace-Mann-Lincoln Institute of School Experimentation, Teachers College, Columbia University. My colleagues on the project, Paula Holzman, Harvey Hornstein, and Dale Lake stimulated many of the ideas recorded here, and gave critical reading to the manuscript.

References

Argyris, C. *Integrating the Individual and the Organization.* New York: Wiley, 1964.

——————. *Interpersonal Competence and Organizational Effectiveness.* Homewood, Ill.: Dorsey Press, 1962.

Barton, A. H. and Wilder, D. E. "Research and Practice in the Teaching of Reading: A Progress Report." In M. B. Miles (Ed.), *Innovation in Education.* New York: Bureau of Publications, Teachers College, Columbia University, 1964. Pp. 361-398.

Bennis, W. G. "Towards a 'Truly' Scientific Management: The Concept of Organization Health." In A. Rapaport (Ed.), *General Systems.* (Yearbook of the Society for the Advancement of General Systems Theory). Ann Arbor, Michigan: 1962.

——————. "A New Role for the Behavioral Sciences: Effecting Organizational Change." *Administrative Science Quarterly,* 1963, 8 (2), 125-165.

——————. "Theory and Method in Applying Behavioral Science to Planned Organizational Change." Cambridge: Alfred P. Sloan School of Management, M.I.T., 1964. Mimeographed.

..............., Benne, K. D., and Chin, R. *The Planning of Change: Readings in the Applied Behavioral Sciences.* New York: Holt, Rinehart and Winston, 1961.

Blake, R. R., Blansfield, M. G., and Mouton, J. S. "How Executive Team Training Can Help You." *Journal American Society of Training Directors*, 1962, *16* (1), 3-11.

Burns, T. and Stalker, G. M. *The Management of Innovation.* London: Tavistock Publications, 1961.

Callahan, R. E. and Button, H. W. "Historical Change of the Role of the Man in the Organization, 1865-1950." In D. E. Griffiths (Ed.), *Behavioral Science and Educational Administration.* Sixty-third Yearbook (Part II), National Society for the Study of Education. Chicago: University of Chicago Press, 1964.

Carlson, R. O. "School Superintendents and the Adoption of Modern Math: A Social Structure Profile." In M. B. Miles (Ed.), *Innovation in Education.* New York: Bureau of Publications, Teachers College, Columbia University. Pp. 329-342.

Clark, J. V. "A Healthy Organization." Los Angeles, California: Institute of Industrial Relations, University of California, 1962.

Gage, N. L. "A Method for 'Improving' Teacher Behavior." *Journal of Teacher Education*, 1963, *14* (3), 261-266. (a)

..............., (Ed.) *Handbook of Research on Teaching.* Chicago: Rand McNally, 1963. (b)

Gallaher, A. "The Role of the Advocate and Directed Change." Paper presented at the Symposium on Identifying Techniques and Principles for Gaining Acceptance of Research Results of Use of Mass Media in Education. Lincoln, Nebraska: November 24-27, 1963.

Golembiewski, R. "Authority as a Problem in Overlays." *Administrative Science Quarterly*, 1964, *9* (1), 23-49.

Jahoda, M. *Current Concepts of Positive Mental Health.* New York: Basic Books, 1958.

Likert, R. *New Patterns of Management.* New York: McGraw-Hill, 1961.

Lippitt, R., Watson, J. and Westley, B. *The Dynamics of Planned Change.* New York: Harcourt, Brace, 1958.

Lortie, D. C. "Craftsmen and Colleagueship, A Frame for the Investigation of Work Values Among Public School Teachers." Paper read at American Sociological Association meetings, 1961.

Mann, F. C. "Studying and Creating Change." In W. G. Bennis, K. D. Benne, and R. Chin, *The Planning of Change: Readings in the Applied Behavioral Sciences.* New York: Holt, Rinehart and Winston, 1961. Pp. 605-615.

Maslow, A. "Self-actualizing People: A Study of Psychological Health." In W. Wolff (Ed.), *Personality Symposium.* New York: Grune and Stratton, 1950. Pp. 11-34.

Miles, M. B. *Innovation in Education.* New York: Bureau of Publications, Teachers College, Columbia University, 1964. (a)

..............., "On Temporary Systems." In M. B. Miles (Ed.) *Innovation in Education.* New York: Bureau of Publications, Teachers College, Columbia University, 1964. (b) Pp. 437-492.

Morse, N. and Reimer, E. "The Experimental Change of a Major Organizational Variable," *Journal of Abnormal and Social Psychology*, 1956, *52*, 120-129.

Peterson, W. A. "Age, Teacher's Role, and the Institutional Setting." In B. J. Biddle and W. J. Ellena (Eds.), *Contemporary Research on Teacher Effectiveness.* New York: Holt, Rinehart and Winston, 1964. Pp. 264-315.

Rogers, E. M. *Diffusion of Innovations.* New York: Free Press, 1962.

Ross, D. H. (Ed.) *Administration for Adaptability.* New York: Metropolitan School Study Council, 1958.

Schachtel, E. G. *Metamorphosis.* New York: Basic Books, 1959.

Sieber, S. D. "The School Board as an Agency of Legitimation." *Sociology of Education,* in press. Bureau of Applied Social Research Reprint No. A-404, Columbia University.

Warriner, C. J. "Groups are Real: A Reaffirmation. *American Sociological Review,* 1956, *21,* 549-554.

Zand, D., Miles, M. B., and Lytle, W. O. Jr. "Organizational Improvement Through Use of a Temporary Problem-Solving System." In D. E. Zand and P. C. Buhanan, (Eds.), *Organization Development: Theory and Practice.* Forthcoming.

Zander, A. (Ed.) *Performance Appraisals: Effects on Employees and Their Performance.* Ann Arbor, Michigan: Foundation for Research on Human Behavior, 1963.

3

Directed Change
in
Formal Organizations:
The School System

By
ART GALLAHER, JR.

Directed Change in Formal Organizations: The School System

ART GALLAHER, JR.
University of Kentucky

IN THE PAPER that follows I shall examine certain limited phenomena and raise a number of issues that seem relevant—always from the viewpoint of an anthropologist—and I shall make a number of suggestions which, when recast in your own frame of reference, will serve as positions for discussion. I propose to do this by first examining the nature of change as it is viewed by anthropologists. In this discussion I will emphasize the role of advocate because I believe it is crucial. This will be followed by an examination of the concept "formal organization," with some attention turned on the organizational peculiarities of the school and the implications of these for understanding directed educational change. I shall then comment briefly on what seems to me the crucial problem before the seminar—the potential of the school administrator in the role of advocate.

THE NATURE OF CHANGE

When the anthropolgist talks of change he speaks of change in culture because the latter, more than any other concept, focuses the great number of diverse interests which characterize anthropology as a behavioral science. By culture is meant those ideas, socially transmitted and learned, shared by the members of a group and toward which in their behavior they tend to conform.[1] Culture, then, provides the selective guidelines—ways of feeling, thinking, and reacting—that distinguish one group from another. This is true whether by group we refer to large social systems, such as nation-state societies, or, more relevant for our purposes, to smaller social systems, formal organiza-

---

[1] For the many ways in which culture has been defined by anthropologists and other behavioral scientists, see A. L. Kroeber and Clyde Kluckhohn, *Culture: A Critical Review of Concepts and Definitions.* Papers of the Peabody Museum, Vol. XLVII, No. 1, Harvard University, 1952. This volume lists some 160 definitions and groups these according to the qualities of culture that are emphasized. This particular work demonstrates what a tremendously rich and fluid concept culture really is.

tions such as a hospital, a labor union, or a school system in a given community. As a convenient way of denoting a lower level of conceptual abstraction, the latter are sometimes called "subcultures."

The preoccupation with culture by anthropologists rests on a number of basic premises, two of which are especially germane to our interests in this seminar. One is the belief held by anthropologists that culture, since it is socially transmitted and learned, and since it is a major adaptive mechanism of man, is bound to change.[2] Very early in their empirical data anthropologists became aware of the *normative* quality of culture, that is, in a given social situation the carriers of a culture can define the *ideal* behavior pattern that is called for. It was apparent just as early, too, that there were gaps between the ideal and the *actual* patterns of behavior. The significance of this finding ultimately led to the premise that a given culture is bound to change with time because 1) man's adjustment to his non-human environment is never fully complete, what Wilbert Moore calls *the constant environmental challenge*,[3] and 2) no known group is free from social deviation though such information does not always find its way into the monographs written by anthropologists. If we want to view this in a slightly different way, the sociocultural systems developed by man are tension-producing as well as tension-reducing, and the attempts to manage tension are productive of innovation and its acceptance.[4] I am, therefore, suggesting that a tension-management organizational model is useful for culture change purposes because, among other reasons, it implies the viewpoint that change is a natural consequence of human social life.

Though it was recognized early in anthropology that changes in culture could be internally derived, as through *invention* and *discovery*, the greater attention by far has been paid to changes that accompany contact between groups. Two of the more important concepts developed to explain contact change are *diffusion*,[5] which refers to the

---

[2] This belief has not always characterized anthropology; many of the early field-workers, who studied mainly isolated societies, accepted a model of culture as essentially stable. However, as culture came to be understood better this interpretation proved so inadequate that some theorists asserted the other extreme, that every culture is, in fact, in a constant and continuous state of change. Without qualification, the latter position is as misleading as the former. Most contemporary anthropologists would accept Keesing's suggestion as more in line with the facts; that is, "Proper perspective on this problem must see forces making both for stability and change." See Felix M. Keesing, *Cultural Anthropology*, Rinehart & Co., New York, 1958, p. 384.

[3] In an unpublished paper titled "Developmental Change in Urban-Industrial Societies." This paper will be published in a volume of essays on Developmental Change, edited by Art Gallaher, Jr.

[4] Ibid.

[5] Diffusion in Anthropology has been concerned mainly with the distribution of elements of culture as opposed to a concern with diffusion as process. The latter is much more identified with rural sociologists. See Everett M. Rogers, *Diffusion of Innovations*, The Free Press of Glencoe, New York, 1962, for a

transfer of culture elements from one group to another, and *acculturation*,[6] which refers to changes occurring in the culture of one group in contact with another. Out of the research focused on these two concepts came the distinction between *non-directed* and *directed* culture change.[7] It is the latter, of course, that is important to us.

By directed culture change is meant a structured situation in which an advocate interferes actively and purposefully with the culture of a potential acceptor. In this situation an advocate consciously selects elements in a *target system* (that which is to be changed) and by stimulating the acceptance of innovations, inhibiting the practice of prior patterns of behavior, or, as is frequently the case, doing both of these things simultaneously, he manages the direction of change. The success with which this is done depends mainly on 1) how the advocate plays his role, particularly his use of authority, and 2) the behavior of those who make up the target system. We shall return to the matter of change shortly, but before talking of the second major premise that we need to have in mind, let me emphasize that I believe the way that the advocate plays his role is one of the more crucial variables in the success or failure of attempts to direct change.

A second premise regarding the nature of culture that is particularly important to us is the belief held by anthropologists that parts of a culture, however conceptualized, are linked to other parts and, therefore, any element of culture is comprehended fully only by understanding its relationship to other simultaneously present, relevant facts. This is, of course, the *structural-functional* viewpoint,[8] and

---

good statement by a rural sociologist; see also Herbert F. Lionberger, *Adoption of New Ideas and Practices,* Iowa State University Press, 1960. For a statement by an anthropologist, see the last three chapters of Ralph Linton, *Acculturation in Seven American Indian Tribes.* Appleton-Century Co., New York, 1940. A number of other general works in anthropology, published during the 1930's and later, include sections of diffusion.

6 Acculturation is one of the major concepts used by anthropologists in their studies of change process. One of the first attempts to systematize the concept was by a Social Science Research Council Sub-Committee on Acculturation, composed of Melville Herskovits, Robert Redfield, and Ralph Linton. The results of the seminar were published in 1937 and were recently made available again under the original title, *Acculturation: The Study of Culture Contact,* by Peter Smith, Publisher, Gloucester, Mass., 1958. The bibliographic reference is to Melville J. Herskovits. Another Social Science Research Council Seminar grappled with the concept in 1953. The results of that seminar are reported as "Acculturation: An Exploratory Formulation" in the *American Anthropologist,* Vol. 56, No. 6, Pt. 1, 1954, pp. 973-1003. Another useful publication is *Acculturation Abstracts,* edited by Bernard Siegel. Stanford University Press, 1955.

7 For an early statement regarding this distinction, see Ralph Linton, *Acculturation in Seven American Indian Tribes,* op. cit. ch. 10. For a more recent statement on types of contact change, see Edward H. Spicer, "Types of Contact and Processes of Change" in *Perspectives in American Indian Culture Change,* edited by E. H. Spicer, University of Chicago Press, 1961.

8 This refers to the basic premise of functionalism. For an excellent summary of the concept see Raymond Firth's "Function," in *Current Anthropology,* edited

if we keep in mind that the interdependence of parts that is implied is not absolute but is rather a matter of degree, it is a view that is not only useful but one that I believe necessary for understanding the full ramifications of change processes.[9] In line with this, the distinction between manifest and latent functions is especially relevant for understanding directed sociocultural change situations.[10] I say this because, in directed change, purpose should be made explicit, and it is precisely at the manifest-latent level of analysis that we confront directly the matter of purpose. By manifest function we shall refer to those objective, hence intended, consequences of whatever part of culture we define; by latent we shall refer to the unintended and unrecognized consequences of the same order.[11] For example, in a rural community that I once did research in I found that the manifest function of membership on the school board was to serve the school by working with the superintendent in budget and other policy matters. At the same time, a latent function of membership on the board was the acquisition of a kind of political power that had nothing whatsoever to do with education, but which, when exercised, was very often detrimental to the manifest objectives of the school system.

We can now turn our attention to some of the variables viewed by anthropologists as influencing the acceptance or ultimate rejection of innovation. In order to facilitate our understanding of these variables let me first introduce a conceptual framework within which we can perceive them as related. In this regard it will be useful for us to have in mind what is meant by a *culture change cycle*. The latter is viewed by anthropologists as involving three broadly conceived processes. These are: 1) *innovation*, the process whereby a new element of culture or combination of elements is made available to a group; 2) *dissemination*, the process whereby an innovation comes to be shared; and 3) *integration*, the process whereby an innovation becomes mutually adjusted to other elements in the system.[12] In our discussion here, attention will focus mainly on the more significant concepts and variables by which we understand innovation and dissemination.

Homer Barnett, who has authored the most extensive anthropological treatise on innovation, sees it as a mental process, and makes the point that every man is a potential innovator. Barnett is concerned es-

by William L. Thomas, Jr., University of Chicago Press, 1955. See also Laura Thompson, *Toward a Science of Mankind*, McGraw-Hill Co., 1961, p. 9. Also, see Harry Johnson, *Sociology*, Harcourt, Brace and Co., New York, 1960, pp. 48-63.

[9] See Robert K. Merton, *Social Theory and Social Structure*, Free Press, 1957, pp. 25 et seq., and Alvin W. Gouldner, "Reciprocity and Autonomy in Functional Theory," in L. Z. Gross, Ed., *Symposium on Social Theory*, Row, Peterson, 1958.

[10] Neal Gross makes this point for educational sociology in "The Sociology of Education," in Robert Merton, et. al. (eds.) *Sociology Today*, Basic Books, 1959.

[11] See Robert K. Merton, op cit., pp. 61-66.

[12] Ralph Linton, op. cit., last three chapters.

sentially with the creative act of innovation, and he turns most of his attention on delineating the cultural and psychological variables which underlie specific innovative processes.[13] I do not believe, however, that our concern in this seminar is in that direction. Rather, we are more concerned with the introduction of changes in ways that will best gain their acceptance. It will be useful for us, then, to distinguish between the term *innovator*, which we will reserve for the individual or agency responsible for the conception of an innovation, and *advocate*, which we shall use to refer to individuals or agencies who sponsor an innovation for the express purpose of gaining its acceptance by others.[14] Thus, in the directed change situation we can assume that the role of advocate is always a purposive one. With these few comments out of the way, we can turn our attention to some of the variables which influence the definition and enactment of the advocacy role.

Elsewhere I have suggested that there are two major role models for advocacy,[15] that the distinction between these is one of means rather than ends, and that in each case the conception of means for gaining acceptance derives from assumptions about the nature of change. The model that I call the *pragmatic advocate* prescribes a role concerned mainly with creating a climate conducive to acceptance; the view of the culture change cycle is global, acceptance is to be achieved, but the *processes of acceptance* are accorded signal importance. This model rests on the premise that success or failure in directed change is referable mainly to the advocate's understanding of the content and internal organization of the pattern where change is sought.

The *Utopic model* defines the advocate's role mainly as one of manipulation to gain the acceptance of an innovation; the view of the culture change cycle is myopic, it focuses almost exclusively on the *act of acceptance*. There is a basic premise that one can achieve results best by doing things to, or planning for, people rather than with them.

For most cases I believe the pragmatic model is the best for achieving genuine change; that is, acceptance that is valued. I believe it is best because it is based on complete and detailed knowledge of the target system, and in the directed change situation there is no substitute for that. There is, in fact, a large body of research to support the basic assumptions underlying the pragmatic model, that is that people will more readily accept innovations that they can understand

[13] Homer Barnett, *Innovation: The Basis of Culture Change.* McGraw-Hill Co., New York, 1953, especially chapters 2-6.

[14] Ibid., pp. 291-295.

[15] Art Gallaher, Jr., "The Role of the Advocate and Directed Change." Paper read at the University of Nebraska Symposium on Identifying Techniques and Principles for Gaining Acceptance of Research Results. To be published in a volume edited by Wes Mierhenry.

and perceive as relevant,[16] and secondly, that they have had a hand in planning.[17] Working from this model, and with these two assumptions in mind, the task of the advocate is made easier if he is prestigeful in ways that are valued by the target system. Related to the matter of prestige, and very often a function of it, is the more important variable of the *dependence upon authority*[18] that is shared in the target system. This is a simple and practical matter of the following order: in a given community are potential acceptors willing to adopt an innovation in the public school system advocated by a school administrator, or will they follow the lead of a physician or a political pressure group of "super-patriots," or other source of opposition? Who are those who command some kind of authority and who, because of it, can be expected to serve logically as emulative models in the dissemination of an innovation?

In the directed change situation I believe that dependence upon authority is one of the more crucial variables. I would urge those who must plan educational change in our society to give careful consideration to the kinds of authority to which innovations are tied. It may be that conventional authorities already present are inadequate. We may need to invent new ones, and with the assistance of mass media and other devices by which we manage such things, endow them with the kind of prestige and other qualities necessary to get the job done.

Viewed in a different way, the matter of authority assumes added relevance. If we view authority as the control that some members in the group have over the activities of others, it follows that those with rank and power in an organization control rewards. Rewards are, in fact, a major mediating factor in the reciprocity that characterizes the social relationship of those with power and those without it. Stated bluntly, those in authority can sometimes effect change by denying customary reciprocity; that is, by manipulating rewards in ways that deny the target system an expected gratification.[19] We must

---

[16] The list of sources is long. The following, taken from research done in management and industry, support this hypothesis. Robert A. Goodwin and Charles A. Nelson (eds.), *Toward the Liberally Educated Executive*, the New American Library, New York, 1960; Auren Uris, *The Management Makers*, The MacMillan Co., New York, 1962, pp. 91-164; Harold Koontz and Cyril O'Donnell, *Principles of Management*, McGraw-Hill Book Co., Inc., New York, 1959, pp. 359-385.

[17] Again, the list of sources to support this hypothesis is long. A representative sample would include the following: Georges Friedman, *Industrial Society*, The Free Press, Glencoe, Ill., 1955, pp. 261-372; Kurt Lewin, "Group Decision and Social Change," in T. Newcomb and E. Hartley (eds.), *Readings in Social Psychology*, Henry Holt and Co., New York, 1949, pp. 330-344; Edward H. Spicer, *Human Problems in Technological Change*, Russell Sage Foundation, 1952, cases 7, 8, 11, 14.

[18] Homer Barnett, op. cit., Ch. 3, for a discussion of this variable in connection with innovation.

[19] For a good discussion of this point see Charles P. Loomis, "Tentative Types of Directed Social Change Involving Systemic Linkage," *Rural Sociology*, Vol. 24, No. 4, Dec., 1959, pp. 383-390.

keep in mind, however, that the distinction between those with authority and those without it is not always clearly defined; in a given organization there may exist checks and balances on the definitions and use of authority. In this regard, Howard Becker's research on the authority systems of the public school is very interesting.[20] So far as the professional functionaries are concerned, and here we are talking of administrators and teachers, each controls sanctions that permit some control over the other's behavior. However, I shall later make the point that authority in the educational organization, because its goal is service, derives its significance more at that point where the organization articulates with the client group.

There is another variable that I should like to stress as especially crucial in the success of an advocate in a directed change situation and that is *the expectation of change*[21] shared by members of the target system. It is important for an advocate to know the areas of culture where people value change and where they have come to expect it. These are channels into which innovations can be fed with the greatest chance of success. On the other hand, if such expectations are not present, or if innovations cannot be tailored to fit those that are, the advocate may find their creation essential to his long-range task. In line with this, an important quality for the target system to have is the capacity for criticism.[22] It may well be that this capacity is not present, and that it will have to be encouraged. A corollary that the advocate should keep in mind here, however, is that the *margin of security* for many in the target system may be very low, hence an alternative in the form of an innovation becomes doubly threatening. This is somewhat contrary to the long-held view that those who derive security from an organization are reluctant to change the vehicle of their success. I am suggesting that in formal organizations of a service variety, such as educational systems are, the opposite might well be true—those who are secure can sustain the threat of examining alternatives, whereas those whose margin of security is low will resist changing a system that has *accommodated to them*. In practical terms, within our present frame of reference, I am posing the hypothesis that the better teachers in a given school system are more likely to accept innovations than are the poorer ones; the more educationally secure members of the client group are more likely to accept innova-

[20] "The Teacher in the Authority System of the Public School," in Amitai Etzioni (ed.) *Complex Organizations: A Sociological Reader*, Holt, Rinehart, and Winston, New York, 1961, pp. 243-255.

[21] Homer Barnett, op. cit., Chapter 2 for a discussion of "expectation of change" as a cultural variable in innovation.

[22] See Margaret Mead, "Changing Culture: Some Observation in Primitive Societies," in *The Human Meaning of the Social Sciences*, edited by Daniel Lerner, Meridian Books, 1959. In this article Dr. Mead explores the variables which cause people to reflect on culture change.

tions in the system than those who are less familiar with the intricacies of the educational process.

A number of other variables that influence the acceptance and rejection of innovation involve the general matter of *scale*. For example, what is the extent of the target system's *felt need* for change? Is the *time factor* right; that is, is the system already undergoing change, or is there a target system apathy induced by previous innovative failures? There is also the matter of size in the system to be changed, and the associated organizational complexity that varies with size. The latter bears importantly on communications effectiveness, which in turn relates to the problem of determining the most viable unit for effecting change. It might be that even when the entire target system is scheduled for change, it can be done best by changing smaller, more manageable components one at a time.

One further point regarding communications should be emphasized and that is, the advocate in his concern with the formal properties of communication systems should not ignore the informal, less structured channels for moving information. In formal organizations the social cliques that develop among work associates or around some other common interest can be invaluable channels for communicating information *so that it will be accepted*.

The Nature of Formal Organizations

By formal organization we shall mean one that is deliberately conceived and planned for the explicit purpose of achieving certain goals. All organizations have social structure and they can be viewed as subcultures. If they are of any considerable size the most significant aspects of social structure are typically a centralized authority and an ordered status hierarchy. Viewed as a subculture, the formal organization has at minimum a normative system that defines the purpose, the *goal-orientation*, of the personnel who occupy the specialized statuses and perform specialized roles within the organization. At its most formal level the dimensions of the subculture are prescribed in the organization's official body of rules. Though the structural and cultural aspects of organization seem obvious, we must make sure that they are not so obvious that we lose sight of them. In directed change especially we should continually explicate these two dimensions and keep them conceptually separate. We must know which we plan to change. For example, do we want to modify structure to more efficiently attain goals in the system, or do we want to maintain a structure and innovate new goals? Above all, an advocate must never assume that change in one aspect will necessarily lead to desired change in the other. Depending on the organization in a change situation, culture and social structure may each manifest peculiarly stubborn strains toward autonomy.

So far as directed change is concerned, those aspects of formal organization that are most important are the authority that we attach to the structure and, from a cultural standpoint, the matter of a goal-orientation and normative procedures for arriving at defined goals. The dimension of authority which has received the most attention in the formal organization literature is legitimation. The latter, which can be crucial in directed change situations, has been a topic of some concern by social scientists, especially since Max Weber addressed himself to the subject. Weber believed that authority in organizations is legitimated in three ways: 1) by the sanctity of tradition, 2) by values that derive from conceptions of the divine or supernatural power (the Charismatic leader), and 3) by a belief in the supremacy of the law.[23]

There is no need for us to elaborate these categories here. Rather, we can agree with Gouldner[24] when he says:

"The authority of the modern administrator is characteristically legitimated on the basis of his specialized expertise; that is, administrators are regarded as proper incumbents of office on the basis of what they know about the organization or their professional skills, rather than whom they know."

Since we have suggested earlier that the tension-management model is a good one for understanding the dynamics of change, it is interesting to note here that Gouldner[25] also sees the problems surrounding authority as constituting a major factor in organizational tension.

From the standpoint of directed change the matter of authority in formal organizations derives its importance from factors other than mere legitimation. For example, in a formal organization what statuses are most likely to be extended to encompass the advocacy role? A logical hypothesis is that statuses with the most authority legitimated around the goals of an organization are the ones that advocacy responsibility is most likely to be attached to. Among other things, such statuses presumably have more sanctions vested in them than do others. However, successful innovation often is achieved only in the absence of formal sanctions, in which case persuasion or other methods are employed. Therefore, viewed from the perspective of the target system we need to ask the following: does the target system view the role of authorities legitimated by the functional requirements of the organization as including also the responsibility for innovation? They may not. In fact, their perception of the legitimated authority's role set may emphasize the opposite so strongly that they

[23] See H. H. Gerth and C. Wright Mills (trans. and eds.), *From Max Weber: Essays in Sociology*, New York, Oxford University Press, 1946, pp. 196-204.
[24] Alvin W. Gouldner, "Organizational Analysis," in Robert K. Merton, et. al. (eds.), *Sociology Today*, Basic Books, New York, 1959, pp. 413.
[25] Ibid., pp. 413-416.

will not tolerate a redefinition of it to include innovative responsibility. Those who direct change in formal organizations should keep in mind the formal properties of a system do not tell the whole story; in the matter of authority just mentioned, for example, recipients can and do organize in ways that enable them to resist pressures placed by formal authority.

It seems appropriate at this point, then, to emphasize that the formal aspects of social structure and culture which characterize an organization are always accompanied by networks of informal relations and unofficial norms. The informal relations that emerge are, of course, related to the nature of the organization and they, in turn, mold the behavior of functionaries in ways which obviously influence the formal properties of the system. In short, there are in all formal organizations elements of structure that are organizationally unprescribed, such as cliques and informal status structures, but which are not unrelated to the formal elements of structure. For example, a clique of work associates can easily resist pressures placed on them to increase production, accept innovations, and the like,[26] and it is a fortunate school administrator, indeed, who has not had to contend with the passive resistance techniques of teachers.[27] We know group cohesiveness to be one of the most important aspects of the informal structure.

Concomitant with the informal structures are elements of culture, that is, patterns of belief and sentiment, that are also organizationally unprescribed. For example, in a given school system there is every likelihood that one will find the unofficial norm that one teacher must never question another's grade, even if it is known that the grade is unjustified. To do so is to threaten the authority system that the teachers are attempting to define.[28] Again, it is worth reiterating that those who direct change in formal organizations will find it imperative to have knowledge of both the formal and informal aspects of the target system.

Another feature of formal organizations that must always be kept in mind is that they never exist in a social vacuum, but rather are linked to other organizations in a larger social system. From an analytical viewpoint we must, then, establish the parameters within which the formal organization derives its significance; that is, the boundaries within which authority is legitimated, goals are defined, and decisions are made. It is important to keep in mind that there is no inherent congruity between these three levels of action; one may rest on the local autonomy of the organization itself, whereas the other two may derive significance mainly from the external environment.

---

[26] See especially F. J. Roethlisberger and William J. Dickson, *Management and the Worker*, Cambridge, Mass., Harvard University Press, 1939.

[27] Howard K. Becker, "The Teacher in the Authority System of the Public School," op. cit.

[28] Ibid.

In a very worthwhile article on organizational analysis, Gouldner[29] casts linkage not in the conceptual framework of integration of the parts, but rather from the vantage point of "the functional autonomy of organizational parts." Again, with our tension management model in mind, he offers the interesting hypothesis that " . . . the structure of complex organizations . . . serves to maintain and protect the parts from others within the same system, at least in some degree. Thus organizational structure is shaped by a tension between centrifugal and centripetal pressures, limiting as well as imposing control over parts, separating as well as joining them." More than any other formal organization that I can presently think of, an understanding of the adjustment of the school to its external environment is crucial for those who would guide us to innovations in education.[30] This becomes even more relevant when we understand some of the peculiar qualities that characterize the school system as a formal organization. I am referring to the peculiarities associated with the two aspects for formal organization—authority and the establishment and maintenance of goals—that I have identified as crucial in directed change. We now turn our attention to these considerations.

COMMENTS ON THE SCHOOL SYSTEM AS A FORMAL ORGANIZATION

Viewed from a global perspective, the most significant quality of the school as a formal organization to keep in mind is that it is a *service organization*.[31] This means that the prime beneficiary of the organization is the client group, which in turn becomes a crucial variable in determining the limits and kinds of authority that are developed, and the goal orientation that the organization will take.

The professional functionaries in the school, that is administrators and teachers, confront continually the dilemma of legitimating their authority to determine goals in the system.[32] By all of the rights of passage, whether administrator or teacher, theirs is a specialized expertise that presumably equips them to determine the client beneficiaries' own best interests. However, I believe we should have to look long and hard to find a client group—those served by hospital, mental health, social work organizations, to name a few—that more agressively questions professional authority than the one served by education. This is not new, it is a traditional matter. With a wide spectrum of values to draw from, many of which are anti-intellectual and not the least of which is local autonomy, the client group has, indeed, in-

[29] Alvin W. Gouldner, 1959, op. cit.

[30] Neal Gross, op. cit., makes the point that this is an area that needs research by those interested in the sociology of education.

[31] Peter M. Blau and W. Richard Scott, *Formal Organizations*, Chandler Publishing Company, San Francisco, 1962, Chapter 2.

[32] Ibid, pp. 51-54. The point is made that service organizations commonly face the problem of becoming captives of the client group.

sisted upon a system which permits formal control to rest in the hands of laymen.[33] This control is given its most explicity symbolic representation in that major structural link between the school and its external environment, including the client group itself, the school board. As Gross[34] suggests, we need to understand this phenomenon better. For example, if the manifest function of a school board is to establish policies governing a local public-school system, what are the latent functions of a school board? It is not hard to receive the impression in many communities that the board has as its main function the protection of the community from the schools.

It is true that the power to legitimate authority and to establish goals is not as much in the local community or school district today as formerly. Much, in fact, has been relinquished to the state. However, enough is there to make this one of the very real problems for planning educational change. This is true because *so many problems currently defined in local school systems, and the innovations necessary to solve them, today owe their relevance to larger systems, such as the region or the nation-state*, more than at any prior period in our history. At the same time, because of racial integration, the prayer decision, and other political developments in our society, there is the greatest possible concern with local autonomy. There are, in fact, disturbing reports from teachers in all sections of the country that their professional status is increasingly threatened, especially by reactionary political elements that hope to reduce alternative goals in education. The client group's new and vigorous interest in local autonomy could not come at a time when it is more out of touch with the sociocultural reality in which education must find its place. This seemingly paradoxical situation—*the concern of local client groups in the power to legitimate authority, a centrifugal tendency, contrasted to the centripetal one of problems in the local system, and the innovations necessary to solve them, deriving from larger systems—could well be the most difficult problem area for educational innovators*. Its importance should not be underestimated.

The task of professional functionaries is probably more difficult in service organizations than in any other kind. They must serve the collective interests of the client group and at the same time retain their authority and not become subservient to the demands of the client group.[35] I need only remind you that surrender to the client is not unknown in education. Many administrators and teachers take the line of least resistance and there are cases known where systems have surrendered to the client group.[36]

---

[33] This point is also made by Neal Gross, op. cit., p. 137. He suggests this as an area that needs research in the sociology of education.

[34] Ibid., p. 133.

[35] Peter M. Blau and W. Richard Scott, op. cit., pp. 51-54.

[36] See especially Burton R. Clark, *Adult Education in Transition: A Study of Institutional Insecurity*, University of California Press, 1956.

From the positive side, though, educational planners can derive some comfort from the knowledge that traditionally Americans have kept a kind of flexibility in their thinking about education and certainly a predisposition to change content and method. I am not sure that this predisposition to weigh alternatives is so evident when goals are involved, but then the latter are not always explicit. We might, in fact, say that more attention should be given to explicating viable goals in education, especially if we are to turn more of our attention on planning for change. Nevertheless, the process of education has been tied one way or another to related considerations of change, such as the dominant concern with social mobility, and this has led to something of an expectation of change in education. Those who direct innovations should be alert to this and, whenever possible, take advantage of it. Again, a word of caution is in order: the concern for local autonomy that I have mentioned may not permit this expectation of change to carry over into problem areas that derive their significance from beyond the local area or region.

THE SCHOOL ADMINISTRATOR AS ADVOCATE

The research in anthropology points to two classes of people as those most likely to be successful in bringing about change. Barnett,[37] who believes that the essential element in the innovative process is dissatisfaction, suggests four categories of people as innovators; these are also the ones most likely to initially accept an innovation. However, we have distinguished conceptually between the role of innovator and that of advocate and have indicated that it is the latter that concerns us. I would question that the success of the advocate is related to dissatisfaction; rather, it derives more from other qualities and dissatisfaction may or may not be present. As I have already indicated, I am inclined to the view that it is more important for the advocate to have prestige,[38] and/or that members of the target system depend upon his authority in matters of change.[39]

With these few comments out of the way we can turn our attention now on the role of the school administrator as it presently stands, and offer some comment on his potential as an advocate. I am referring, of course, to the generalized status and role of school administrator, recognizing that there are individual exceptions to the rule. If I had to summarize the school administrator's role in one phrase, it would be *he is the man in the middle*.[40] He stands between the client group,

[37] Homer Barnett, "Personal Conflicts and Culture Change," *Social Forces*, Vol. 20, pp. 160-171.

[38] Richard N. Adams, "Personnel in Culture Change: A Test of a Hypothesis," *Social Forces*, Vol. 30, pp. 185-189.

[39] Homer Barnett, *Innovation: The Basis for Culture Change*, McGraw-Hill Book Co., New York, Chapter 3.

[40] For a good discussion of the "man in the middle" see John Useem, John D. Donoghue, and Ruth Hill Useem, "Men in the Middle of the Third Culture," *Human Organization*, Vol. 22, 1963, pp. 169-179.

technically represented by the school board, and professional and other functionaries who comprise the educational system. "He faces towards several different audiences, each with different sets of demands—school boards, parents, parent groups, teachers, and students—as well as other administrators. He has to play his role appropriately in the light of all these demands."[41]

From a functional viewpoint our "man in the middle" has what Spindler[42] calls *a balancing role.*

> "His job is in large part that of maintaining a working equilibrium of at best antagonistically cooperative forces. This is one of the reasons why *school administrators are rarely outspoken protagonists of a consistent and vigorously profiled point of view.* Given the nature of our culture and social system, and the close connection between the public and the schools *he cannot alienate significant segments of that public and stay in business.*" (Italics mine)

Because his role is a balancing one, and because I see nothing in our sociocultural system to indicate that the linkage of the public and the schools will tolerate any other, I have strong reservations that the school administrator status is the one to assign advocacy functions to. I have already indicated that there seems to be a centrifugal tendency toward local autonomy in legitimating authority, and that at the local level the client group traditionally manages authority. *If* the problems in education were those that could be solved at the local level, *if* the client group was capable of structuring innovative procedures for meeting such problems, and *if* the client group maintained its traditional controls, the school administrator would automatically advocate innovations to other functionaries because of his position in the status hierarchy of the organization. But the system is not that way, and fortunately so. The problems of the local school, and the solutions to these problems, as we have indicated, come from centripetal forces that are pulling each local system out of its environment and into systems that are broader in scale. The sources of local client-centered authority may not be aware of the significance of the larger system or, what is worse, may not even care or resist the fact that it exists. Under these conditions they are not apt to permit advocacy as part of the administrative role. And since the role of advocate is purposive and one that involves commitment that, even under the best of change circumstances, sometimes involves conflict, the school administrator might reduce his balancing role effectiveness if he assumes advocacy. I do not mean the administrator should avoid any concern with change, because that is impossible. Rather, I am asserting that I do not

---

41 George Spindler (ed.), *Education and Culture: Anthropological Approaches,* Holt, Rinehart and Winston, New York, 1963, p. 142.

42 Ibid., p. 238.

believe the problems of change should rest mainly in the administrator's status.

I suggest that we are at an appropriate juncture in our society, meaning that the problems of education viewed from whatever perspective are of sufficient magnitude, to innovate positions that have as their special role function the management of educational change. This could be a special unit called Experimental Education, Planning Division, or by some other innocuous title, built into systems that could afford it. For those that could not meet the expense of such a unit, we should begin to think in terms of a model, perhaps patterned along the lines of agricultural extension. An *educational extension* with a research program focused on creating alternatives and an action program to prepare change agents to assist school systems with innovation, dissemination, and integration problems, is well worth considering. Change is a natural and inevitable consequence of the sociocultural and physical worlds within which our collective lives are acted out and it should be just as natural and just as inevitable that we should give some attention to managing the direction of that change. In line with this, one final word of caution—planning is not something to be taken lightly or as something that just happens; rather, *planning is activity and in and of itself is process.*

4

What Are Innovators Like?

By
EVERETT M. ROGERS

What Are Innovators Like?

Everett M. Rogers

Michigan State University

INNOVATORS ARE the first members of a social system to adopt new ideas.[1] Research studies of farmers, school administrators, industrial firms, and aborigines indicate that they are not always the most respected members of their social system. They prefer venturesomeness to the respect of their peers, who call them "starry-eyed," "experimenters," or people with their "heads in the clouds."[2] Because of their important role in fostering change and their prominence among their peers, innovators are of both theoretical and practical interest. In fact, I would maintain that an understanding the behavior of innovators is essential to a comprehension of the central processes of social change.

PURPOSE

The objective of the present paper is to isolate the characteristics of innovators with special reference to the process of social change. First, however, we must give some attention to how innovators are selected from a total audience that also contains non-innovators.

WHO ARE INNOVATORS?

A great variety of different terms[3] have been used in past research for innovators...

Pioneers
Lighthouses
Advance scouts

[1] Certain ideas in the present paper are similar to Everett M. Rogers, "What Are Innovators Like?" *Theory Into Practice*, 2:252-256, 1963.

[2] Ross, Donald H. (editor), *Administration for Adaptability*, New York: Metropolitan School Study Council, 1958, p. 21. The quoted references are among terms listed by Ross as "only mildly complimentary."

[3] These terms are taken from a review of past research in Everett M. Rogers, *Diffusion of Innovations*, New York: The Free Press of Glencoe, 1962, pp. 150-151.

Progressists
Non-Parochials
Experimentals
Cultural *Avant-garde*

Whatever they are called, there is need for a standard definition of what an innovator is. Because adopter distributions usually appear to approximate a normal, bell-shaped curve over time, I have elsewhere[4] suggested that our standard means of categorizing innovators is to regard them as the first 2.5 per cent of an audience to adopt a new idea. This means they are to the left of the mean ($\overline{X}$) time of adoption minus the standard deviations ($\overline{O}$). Figure 1 shows the position of innovators on the normal adoption curve.

Time-Span of Adoption

Even though the distribution of the adopters of a new idea over time appears to closely approach normality in the cases subject to past

Figure 1

INNOVATORS AS THE FIRST 2.5 PER CENT TO ADOPT A NEW IDEA.

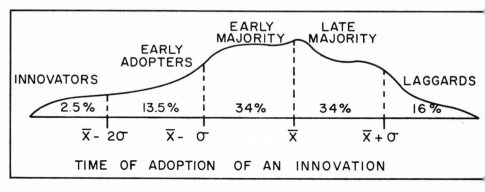

research, the rate of adoption has been found to vary widely in terms of years or some other time-unit. In other words, the period of years from first to last adoption (from extreme left to extreme right in Figure 1) varies widely.

Mort emphasized the relative slowness with which educational practices were adopted by school systems.[5] He found the average school

---

[4] *Op. cit.*, p. 162.
[5] Paul R. Mort, *Principles of School Administration*, N.Y., McGraw-Hill, 1946, pp. 199-200.

". . . lags 25 years behind the best practice." This 50 year time period from first innovator to last laggard may well be a function of the educational practices selected for study, the units of analysis (public high schools), and/or the time of the study (the late 1930's and 1940's). Some educational practices certainly spread more rapidly today. For example . . .

1. Allen compared the diffusion of driver training, an innovation promoted by safety groups and car dealers, with the idea of pupils studying their community.[6] Sixty years were required for this idea to reach 90 per cent adoption among 168 U. S. schools while only 18 years were needed for driver training to reach this level of adoption.

2. Carlson found that "modern math" only required five years to reach about 90 per cent adoption by 43 school superintendents in Allegheny County, Pennsylvania.[7]

In any event, while exact comparison is rather difficult (how equivalent is 2,4-D weed spray to language laboratories to antibiotic drugs?), it appears that our schools change more slowly than our farms, our medical doctors, or our industries. Later in this paper we shall return to discussion of this time-span comparison in terms of implications for school administrators.

Let us first look at what we know about innovators.

A WORD-PICTURE OF THE INNOVATOR

Although, for the present paper, I have drawn primarily on research on the diffusion of innovations in such diverse fields as rural sociology, industrial engineering, and anthropology, I have featured findings on educational innovators when such data are available.

Innovators are venturesome individuals; they desire the hazardous, the rash, the *avant-garde*, and the risky. Since no other model of the innovation exists in the social system, they must also have the ability to understand and use complex technical information. An occasional debacle when one of the new ideas adopted proves to be unsuccesssful does not disquiet innovators. However, in order to absorb the loss of an unprofitable innovation, they must generally have control of substantial financial resources.

Their propensity to venturesomeness brings them out of their local circle of peers and into more cosmopolite social relationships. Even when the geographical distance between them may be considerable,

[6] Harley Earl Allen, *The Diffusion of Educational Practices in the School System of the Metropolitan School Study Council*, D.Ed. Thesis, N.Y., Teachers College, Columbia University, 1956.
[7] Richard O. Carlson, "School Superintendents and Adoption of Modern Math: A Social Structure Profile," in Matthew B. Miles (ed.), *Innovation in Education*, N.Y., Teachers College, Columbia University, Bureau of Publications, 1964, p. 333.

they often have been found to form cliques. They spread new ideas as their gospel.

The description of innovators is sharpened by contrast to that of laggards, who are the last to adopt an innovation (Figure 1). Laggards are localistic; many are near-isolates. Their point of reference is the past, and they interact primarily with those peers who have traditional values like theirs. Laggards tend to be frankly suspicious of innovations, innovators, and change agents. When laggards finally adopt an innovation, it may already be superseded by another more recent idea which the innovators already are using. While innovators look to the road of change ahead, the laggards gaze at the rear-view mirror.

GENERALIZATIONS

Perhaps a meaningful way to more precisely "boil down" the salient characteristics is in terms of a series of generalizations.

1. *Innovators generally are young.* Since the young are less likely to be conditioned by traditional practices within the established culture, there are theoretical grounds for expecting them to be more innovative. Research studies on farmers provide actual evidence that innovators are younger than their peers who are later adopters.

2. *Innovators have relatively high social status, in terms of amount of education, prestige ratings, and income.* Affluence may be indicated by a high income, by ownership of a large-sized operation, or by possession of wealth. Ross reviewed a number of studies dealing with the diffusion of educational ideas among public schools. He concluded that the wealth factor was the one variable most closely related to adoption of innovations.[8]

3. *Impersonal and cosmopolite sources of information are important to innovators.* At the time innovators decide to use a new idea, few members of their social system have had experience with it. As a result, innovators must secure new ideas through impersonal sources, such as the mass media, and from cosmopolite sources, or from outside the social system. Coleman and others found that physicians who innovated were more likely to attend out-of-town medical meetings.[9] Carter and Williams found that innovative industrial firms were more likely to seek new ideas from university researchers.[10]

4. *Innovators are cosmopolite.* The cliques and formal organizations to which they belong are likely to include other innovators. They travel widely and participate in affairs beyond the limits of

---

[8] Ross, *op. cit.*, p. 119.

[9] Coleman, James, Katz, Elihu, and Menzel, Herbert, "The Diffusion of an Innovation among Physicians," *Sociometry*, 20:253-67, 1957.

[10] Carter, C. F., and Williams, B. R., *Industry and Technical Progress*, London; Oxford University Press, 1957.

their system. Ryan and Gross found that hybrid-corn innovators traveled more often to urban centers, such as Des Moines, than did later adopters.[11] Carter and Williams found that in innovative industrial firms "There is extensive world-wide travel by executives, and a lively interest in progress at home and abroad . . ."[12] Ross reported that teachers at more innovative schools usually acquired new educational ideas from outside their community.[13] Goldsen and Ralis found that Thailand farmers who innovate visited Bangkok.[14]

5. *Innovators exert opinion leadership.* Because of their prior experience, innovators obviously are in a position to influence the adoption decision of their peers. Several studies have shown, however, that the norms of the social system may act as an intervening variable between innovativeness and opinion leadership. For example, in communities where the norms were traditional, innovators were not looked to by their peers as sources of information and advice.[15]

6. *Innovators are likely to be viewed as deviants by their peers and by themselves.* Research studies show that farmers who innovate are perceived as deviants from the norms of the social system.

An Ohio study asked what their neighbors thought of their farming methods.[16]

> "Sometimes they shake their heads,"
> "Fifty per cent *think* I am crazy;
> the other 50 per cent are *sure* I am."

Thus, as Thoreau might observe, innovators are in step with a different drummer than their peers; they march to different music.

A composite word-picture of the innovator as represented by the school system is provided by Kumpf:

> "An adaptable school tends to be located in a community which has many people represented in the white-collar or professional occupations, has a high percentage of owner-occupied dwellings, and has many inhabitants 50 years of age or older. It tends to be high in per capita wealth, per pupil expenditure for education, per cent of 8th grade, high school, and college grad-

11 Ryan, Bryce, and Gross, Neal C., "The Diffusion of Hybrid Seed Corn in Two Iowa Communities," *Rural Sociology*, 8:15-24, 1943.

12 Carter, C. F., and Williams, B. R., "The Characteristics of Technically Progressive Firms," *Journal of Industrial Economics*, 7:97, 1959.

13 Ross, *op. cit.*

14 Goldsen, Rose K., and Ralis, Max, *"Factors Related to Acceptance of Innovations in Bang Chan, Thailand,"* Southeast Asia Program Data Paper 25, Ithaca, New York; Cornell University, 1957.

15 Marsh, C. Paul, and Coleman, A. Lee, "Farmers' Practice-Adoption Rates in Relation to Adoption Rates of 'Leaders'," *Rural Sociology*, 19:180-81, 1954.

16 Rogers, Everett M., *"Characteristics of Innovators and Other Adopter Categories,"* Research Bulletin 882, Wooster, Ohio Agricultural Experiment Station, 1961.

uates. A fairly high median (educational level) has been attained by those who are 25 years of age and older in the community. A low percentage of the population is foreign born. It has a high level of understanding of what schools can do. This community is part of a super community which offers many cultural advantages and which contains other schools interested and actively engaged in promoting more adaptable schools.[17]

IMPLICATIONS FOR RESEARCH

Perhaps one implication of the present paper for educational research is that there is not enough of it. Undoubtedly one reason for the relative slowness of educational adoption when compared with agriculture, medicine, or industry is the absence of scientific sources of innovation in education. Chemical companies and the vast network of agricultural experiment stations provide accurate measurements under controlled conditions for a new idea. Farmers, as a result, develop credibility for agricultural research as a source of innovations. Education, on the other hand, has only campus or university schools, and those classes in the nation's schools willing to cooperate in experimentation. Here, first responsibility is to the student, not to research. And the results of educational research are often ambiguous, incomplete and confusing.

I would argue that in conjunction with research to develop educational innovations, we need study of how these new ideas spread and are adopted. Our past research in educational diffusion has been rather unimaginative, and has been the almost sole property of one university. Few studies have been completed with teachers (only one such study was encountered in a search of the literature) as the unit of adoption, and only one study of school superintendents, in spite of their importance in school adoption decisions.

IMPLICATIONS FOR SCHOOL ADMINISTRATORS

Research findings reported in the present paper furnish several implications for school administrators.

1. A high relationship has been found between the financial resources of a school system and its innovativeness. In fact, outstandingly innovative school systems are usually located in particularly wealthy communities.[18] At the same time, however, it is important to remember that not *all* rich schools are innovators and that not *all* schools that innovate are rich. The community's attitude about providing support for the school's costs is obviously an important inter-

17 Kumpf, Carl H., *The Challenge of Studies of Adaptability to an Elementary School in a Large City*, D.Ed. Thesis, Teachers College, Columbia University, 1949, pp. 13-15.

18 Although this is not always true, as Carlson (*op. cit.*, p. 340) has demonstrated. He found a correlation of −.02 between time of adoption of modern math and annual school expenditure per pupil.

vening variable between community wealth and school innovativeness.

As Pelley pointed out, "Unfortunately, there seems to be no possible profit motive in being an educational innovator."[19] The primary motive for more innovative schools must come through the community's desire for more effective learning by their children. However, the amount that learning increases as a result of adopting innovations is difficult to measure. Nevertheless, wherever possible, school administrators should emphasize to the community the results of benefits of educational innovations.

2. The social characteristics, social relationships, and communication behavior of the members of the school staff undoubtedly relate to the innovativeness of their school system. Administrators may create an innovative staff by choosing teachers, possibly young, with breadth of training and cosmopolite sources of information and travel patterns.

3. As the teacher may affect the innovativeness of the school system, so the school system, through its policies, may affect the innovativeness of the teacher. It has been found, for example, that teachers who attend out-of-town educational meetings are more innovative. This suggests that sending teachers to workshops, conferences, and lectures, where they may be exposed to new educational methods, may be a wise investment.

4. The absence of agents that promote change may be a factor in the relative slowness with which schools adopt innovations. Certainly the relatively more rapid adoption of farm innovations is related to the activities of the county extension agent and the agricultural salesman—both important links between agricultural research and the farmer.

The crucial role of school administrators in causing a school to be more or less innovative warrants special emphasis. Innovative school administrators might be expected to maintain close contact with laboratory or experimental schools and with universities through enrollment in graduate work or attendance at conferences and workshops. Demeter concluded, "Building principals are key figures in the process. Where they are both aware of and sympathetic to an innovation, it tends to prosper. Where they are ignorant of its existence, or apathetic if not hostile, it tends to remain outside the blood stream of the school."[20]

---

[19] J. H. Pelley, *Invention in Education*, D.Ed. Thesis, N.Y. Teachers College, Columbia University, 1948, pp. 170-171.

[20] Demeter, Lee H., *Accelerating the Local Use of Improved Educational Practices in School Systems*, D.Ed. Thesis, Teachers College, Columbia University, 1951, p. 23.

5

The Place of Research
in
Planned Change

By
ROLAND J. PELLEGRIN

The Place of Research in Planned Change

Roland J. Pellegrin
University of Oregon

THE TIMES in which we live have been aptly characterized as an era of change. We are confronted today with a world in which rapid changes, far-reaching in scope and significance, impose stresses and strains upon established institutions. In our own society, certain major social trends are forging a social structure radically different from that which existed but a few decades ago. All institutional segments of the society are feeling the impact of these forces. The educational segment is feeling their effects as much as any other.

Education is, in fact, besieged with pressures for change both by external and internal forces. Externally, social conditions and trends call for changes within the field of education. Prominent among these are such diverse matters as automation, technologically induced unemployment, the development of an economy resting on a highly differentiated and specialized division of labor, urbanization, the exploding rate of discovery in many fields of knowledge, the emergence of disadvantaged and alienated segments of the population, and the use of knowledge as a weapon in international struggles. These developments (and others) demand adaptive changes in educational organization and practice.

Within the field of education there are also many pressures for change. There is widespread recognition among educators that there are notable deficiencies and limitations in the content, organization, and administration of the curriculum. At the same time, there has arisen a higher level of aspiration, a feeling that education can increase its contributions to the welfare of society. There is, in short, a belief that changes in education are necessary and desirable, as well as inevitable. But this is but a first step toward coping with the problem of change. There remain serious and complex problems concerning the nature of the changes that should be introduced, the method and timing of their introduction, and so on. In order to cope with such problems, we need much reliable knowledge we do not presently have. How shall we get it?

[65]

The Search for Reliable Knowledge

In seeking answers to this question, it is appropriate that we begin by looking at the various approaches man has developed through the ages in order to "solve" his problems of existence. Man has always had to adapt minimally to his environment; he has always had to cope with uncertainties; he has always been faced with a host of major and minor problems. In other words, man has forever been plagued with the need for knowledge, with the need for controlling his environment.

As we know, he has responded to these needs in a number of ways, developing a variety of approaches to meet the questions and uncertainties that have continually confronted him. We may describe these as follows:[1]

1. *Appeal to the Supernatural.* In our thinking, we usually associate this approach to problem-solving with ancient or primitive peoples. It is true that in our "rational age" few of us seek to analyze, comprehend, and manipulate mystical forces in order to solve our secular problems. Other aspects of this approach remain quite common, however. For example, it is widely assumed that much about what is called "human nature" does not conform to natural laws and is not susceptible to rational analysis. Such thinking views many human problems as insolvable through rational efforts, and relies on faith for amelioration of conditions. Also associated with this approach is an attitude of resignation in the face of problems sometimes accompanied by a hope that if nothing is done the problems will somehow take care of themselves.

2. *Appeal to Worldly Authority.* This approach, of course, relies heavily on tradition, custom, and habitual ways of doing things. Policies and practices are justified on the basis of longevity and persistence, the assumption being made that if something has endured there is good reason to continue it. The approach has many facets. One which remains in common use, for example, is the justification of a practice because it was recommended by a person of high prestige.

3. *Intuition.* This approach assumes that some persons are especially competent to render sound judgments because they are gifted with talent for insight. Intuition is a mysterious process, unclearly related to rational or sensory analysis. The approach is often indistinguishable from the first one we discussed.

4. *Common Sense.* The alleged ability of the individual to reach sound conclusions on the basis of his reasoning capacity and his experience forms the groundwork for this approach. It assumes that the

---

[1] The following classification is found in Stuart Chase, *The Proper Study of Mankind* (Rev. Ed.). New York: Harper and Brothers, 1956, p. 3.

combination of reasoning powers and personal experiences provides sufficient guidelines for action.

5. *Pure Logic.* Of all approaches, this one places the greatest reliance on human faculties as a basis for decision-making. It emphasizes the use of logical reasoning and rational analysis; its primary method is deduction. Reliable knowledge is viewed as the product of logical analysis.

6. *The Scientific Method.* In brief, this approach rests upon the gathering of facts and their analysis by means of induction. It is the only approach that emphasizes the systematic collection of empirical data as the foundation for principles and theory. It is, I believe, the only approach that can provide us with a high probability of success in our search for reliable knowledge. Later on, I shall discuss in some detail the nature of this approach and what we can expect of it. For the moment, however, let me make a few remarks about the other five approaches.

All have a common failing—the percentage of error is quite high. They are but rough guides. While any of these approaches may at times lead to sound conclusions, each is also a road to serious mistakes. None provides a means for checking findings that is based on observed fact.

Each of these approaches can easily be subjected to devastating analysis to demonstrate its deficiencies and inadequacies as a basis for decision-making. I will spare you a detailed analysis, and will content myself with a few comments about one of these approaches, common sense.

As an approach to problem solving, common sense is deficient for a number of reasons. For one thing, the experience of the individual is limited; for another, reasoning ability varies considerably from one person to another. Even more important, however, is the fact that the exercise of common sense suffers from procedural, empirical, and theoretical inadequacies. Stuart Chase had the following comments to make on this subject:

> Eddington, in a famous passage in *Space, Time and Gravitation*, has shown the limitations of common sense. What nonsense, he says, to think that the table on which one writes is a collection of electrons moving with prodigious speed in spaces relatively as empty as the spaces between the planets in the solar system! What nonsense to believe that this thin air presses on every square inch of one's body with a 14-pound weight. What nonsense to think that the light one sees in the eyepiece of this telescope left a star 50,000 years ago.
> Common sense tells us that the world is flat, that the sun goes around the earth, that heavy bodies always fall faster than light bodies, that boats made of iron will sink. The practical man, that

paragon of common sense, was once defined by Disraeli as "one who repeats the errors of his forefathers."[2]

In virtually all spheres of activity, we attempt to solve our problems by falling back on common sense and other defective approaches. This is no less true of education than of most other fields of endeavor. Let us now turn our attention to the bases for decisions, problem-solving, and changes in education.

THE BASES FOR EDUCATIONAL POLICY AND PRACTICE

On what bases do judgments rest in education? What is the rationale underlying existing policies and practices? To what extent do innovations rest on a foundation of reliable knowledge?

In pondering these questions, we cannot fail to be impressed with the extent to which reliance on authority (tradition) is used to justify existing policies and practices, and the extent to which common sense and intuition are used as springboards for innovation. Haskew, in a discussion of approaches to educational improvement, said:

> One traditional answer has been to get as many people as possible to use rational judgment, as best they can, to agree upon (a) what is desirable and (b) what will be likely to bring about the desirable. Another traditional answer is to produce hypotheses of what might be better and to test those hypotheses in some context of evaluative control. A third approach is to investigate and record and then to deduce; deductions may become the basis of planned and directed progress or they merely become subject matter.[3]

All in all, Haskew's evaluation of the foundations of policy and practice is rather charitable. Griffiths, speaking specifically of the field of educational administration, is somewhat caustic in his remarks. "Much of what is now taught," he says, "is composed of the testimonials of successful administrators, the folklore which has accumulated over time, and an odd assortment of 'promising practices.' "[4]

If we continue to focus attention specifically on the field of educational administration, we see that in the intellectual atmosphere that prevails, described by Griffiths as "value bound" and "practice oriented,"[5] a great deal of policy and practice rests on a foundation consisting mainly of ideology and dogma. Hills, in discussing this fact, has

---

[2] *Ibid.*, p. 4.

[3] Lawrence D. Haskew, "A Projective Appraisal," in Daniel E. Griffiths (Ed.), *Behavioral Science and Educational Administration.* The Sixty-third Yearbook of the National Society for the Study of Education, Part II. Chicago: The National Society for the Study of Education, 1964, p. 337.

[4] Daniel E. Griffiths, *Research in Educational Administration: An Appraisal and a Plan.* New York: Bureau of Publications, Teachers College, Columbia University, 1959, p. 5.

[5] *Ibid.*, p. 12.

said that "It seems quite clear that much of what passes for 'good practice' . . . may . . . be considered within the framework of ideology."[6] In substantiating this thesis, Hills asks the reader to examine the following statements, all of which are widely accepted in the field of educational administration. "(1) Experience as a teacher is an essential qualification for an administrator. (2) Schools must be administered democratically. (3) Education must be insulated from politics. (4) School districts must be fiscally independent from municipal governments. (5) Administrators must not fraternize too closely with their subordinates. (6) Administrators must be consistent in their behavior toward teachers. (7) The academically outstanding candidate seldom makes the best classroom teacher. (8) Although he cannot define it, an administrator intuitively knows effective from ineffective teaching. (9) Boards of education should not be organized into standing committees. (10) Established channels of communication must be observed. (11) Males are unsuitable as primary-grade teachers. (12) Males make better administrators than do females. (13) Administrators must back up their teachers in disputes with parents and students, even when the teacher is clearly in the wrong. (14) Primary school children need the security and support provided by having a single teacher for all subjects."[7]

It would be a great exaggeration to say that these statements represent more than agreed-upon assumptions and generalizations. As Hills points out, ". . . these positions are not necessarily wrong. But in most cases, neither is it known that they are right, and that is the essential point. They are, and should be treated as, empirical questions."[8]

Much effort is frequently expended on attempts to achieve goals which are identified through a chain of assumptions resting on a questionable base. One of my favorite examples along these lines is the case of the professionalization movement in education today. Unquestionably, this movement is extremely important in educational circles; in terms of scope and emphasis, it ranks among the most significant recent developments in the field of public education. "Professionalism" among educators is a rallying cry, a symbol of solidarity, and an indicator of attempts to "uplift" the educational enterprise and teaching as an occupation. The term is used to distinguish the dedicated educator from the dilettante, the up-to-date teacher from his dated counterpart, and the loyal educator from the disaffected instructor. The concept of "profession" lies at the heart of current organizational and ideological struggles. Yet there has been almost no empirical study of the functions, meanings, and consequences of these related concepts.

---

[6] R. Jean Hills, "Educational Administration at the Crossroads: The Relevance of the Social Sciences to a Changing Field" (unpublished manuscript), p. 7.

[7] *Ibid.*, pp. 7-8.

[8] *Ibid.*, p. 8.

My intention here is not to speak against professionalization, but to call attention to several matters about the movement. If we examine the literature on professionalization in education, we note at once that the concept itself, despite its universal usage, is vague in meaning and that its behavioral implications are uncertain. It is simply assumed—apparently almost universally—that whatever is done under the banner of professionalization is good. The possibility that there might be dysfunctional consequences to the movement as it is being conducted has apparently been given scant consideration, despite the fact that negative consequences have attended efforts at professionalization in other occupations.[9] Not only has the professionalization movement been subjected to little critical analysis; despite the reams of material published on the subject, there has been virtually no empirical research of any sort done on the matter.

Thus, in this case as in many other examples that could be cited, ideology and untested assumption rule the day. Even worse, some current policy and practice owes its existence to hoary clichés and folk wisdom. A single anecdote will suffice to illustrate this point. Some years ago one of my graduate students and I interviewed an official in charge of vocational education programs in his state. In the course of the conversation, he repeatedly deprecated the state of knowledge pertaining to student selection and training. He emphasized that selection procedures were poor and haphazard; that the goals of the curriculum were often left unachieved; and that virtually nothing was known about student aptitudes and motivations. His conclusion was that the only solution to his problems was research—research designed to give answers to key questions. He waxed eloquent on this subject for quite a while, returning again and again to his two major points, namely, that he and his colleagues were floundering in a sea of ignorance, and that research was the beacon light that could guide them ashore. Finally, he said: "About the only thing we know *for sure* is that in a couple of our training programs all students with red hair are going to flunk out." To our astonished queries he replied that he did not know *why* this was so, but only that it *was* so. Some moments later, one of his subordinates was introduced to us as the director of one of the training programs which those cursed with red hair could not survive. This man had red hair! When I pointed this out to our interviewee, he seemed abashed for a moment, as though he had never noticed his subordinate's affliction. But he recovered quickly, leaned back in his chair, and said triumphantly, "Well! I guess he's the exception that proves the rule, isn't he?"

I do not suggest (perish the thought!) that any substantial segment of educational policy and practice rests on so shaky a foundation. The

---

[9] See, for example, M. Lee Taylor and Roland J. Pellegrin, "Professionalization: Its Functions and Dysfunctions for the Life Insurance Occupation," *Social Forces*, 38 (December, 1959), pp. 110-114.

tale has a moral, however; lacking reliable knowledge, humans will go to any lengths to find a rationale for their actions. The rationale may consist of assumptions and generalizations that *sound* eminently reasonable; it may rest on time-honored practices that extend far into the shadowy past; it may lie firmly embedded in the conventional wisdom of the day. In but relatively few instances, however, does it rest firmly on reliable knowledge.

SCIENTIFIC METHOD, RESEARCH, AND THEORY IN EDUCATION

We now turn attention to how reliable knowledge might be obtained. I see no alternative to empirical research conducted according to the canons of scientific method. In stating this conclusion, however, I recognize that there are tremendous obstacles to overcome before such research can provide the knowledge upon which policy, practice, and innovation in education can rest. The list of these obstacles is long and impressive. Let us take note of some of the principal ones.

Obstacles to Sound Educational Research

1. A major obstacle to research in education is a widespread lack of appreciation for and understanding of the nature and value of research. It can be said with confidence that the general intellectual atmosphere in education is one which gives scant emphasis to the development of a research orientation to one's work, or to the development of a scientific attitude. It goes almost without saying that teachers and administrators rely on precedent and common sense much more than they do on research findings as justifications for their practices. But the problem goes even deeper. There is a common inability to differentiate between fact and opinion. Again and again in reporting research findings to audiences of educators, I have been struck by the fact that many of them equate research findings with opinion and personal experiences—i.e., each of these is viewed as equally good as a source of knowledge. Sometimes the situation is even worse; research findings are regarded as inferior to opinion and precedent. Griffiths reports an experience along these lines. "I was describing the research in pupil-marking and reporting to a group of parents, school administrators, and teachers. As the session proceeded one of the principals became noticeably agitated and finally, unable to restrain himself further, leaped to his feet and said, 'Say, do you believe all this, or is it just research?' "[10]

We have here a vicious circle: (a) many educators do not conceive of the scientific method and research as being of primary significance to their work; (b) this state of mind creates an atmosphere in which low priority is given to the conduct or utilization of research; (c) because of low evaluation and neglect, research continues to be a du-

[10] Griffiths, *Research in Educational Administration: An Appraisal and a Plan,* *op. cit.,* p. 34.

bious enterprise; and (d) because condition (c) exists, condition (a) is perpetuated.

2. Much existing research is low in quality, weak in the insight it imparts, and of dubious utility to the practitioner. Critics have noted a variety of deficiencies, including the following: (a) research has usually avoided crucial problems, focusing instead on topics of minor significance; (b) creativeness has been in short supply, most studies repeating earlier ones in more or less routine fashion; (c) theoretical and conceptual frameworks have been limited, lacking in sophistication, and often unrelated to empirical research; (d) research has been deficient in methodological rigor at all stages in the research process from study design to data analysis; (e) research is not usually cumulative—i.e., the investigator does not build on previous research; and (f) research does not take advantage of the contributions of other disciplines in which relevant work has been done.

3. The nature and functions of "theory" are poorly understood. For many practitioners, the term is a synonym for "wild speculation," an antonym for "practicality." In one survey the urban superintendents of the country were asked to list the outstanding weaknesses of their own programs of graduate study. The one listed most frequently was, "too much theory; courses not practical." Follow-up letters were sent to a sampling of these respondents to find out what they meant by "too theoretical." "The answers to these questions were quite revealing, since they demonstrated many misuses of the word *theory*. Some thought theory was the opposite of practical, thereby equating *theory* with *impractical*. Others had the interesting notion that if a course was *poor*, it was *theoretical* . . . The most common use of the concept theory was as a synonym for *speculation, supposition*, or the *ideal*."[11]

4. There is considerable confusion about the relationship between empirical fact and values. This confusion is seen in the often-heard generalization, "Research can find out what exists, but cannot tell you what value choices you should make." At best this is an over-simplification. The fact of the matter is that reliable knowledge can be used to make intelligent value choices possible, to make us aware of the alternatives among which we might choose. For example, we are now beginning to give a great deal of emphasis to the special educational problems of culturally deprived populations. This choice of emphasis is value-laden. We should also recognize, however, that theoretical formulations and empirical research have called this segment of the population to our attention, have identified the reasons for giving special attention to it, and have pointed out the feasibility and utility

[11] Daniel E. Griffiths, "The Nature and Meaning of Theory," in Griffiths (Ed.), *Behavioral Science and Educational Administration, op. cit.*, p. 96.

of specially designed educational programs. Only in this context could value choices be made as they have been.

5. Research on topics important to education cover a wide range; these topics are complex and difficult to investigate. Yet we have no alternative to tackling these problems head-on. We make no progress by dismissing the task as too difficult or hopeless. Only the research approach gives promise for significant and long-lasting improvements in educational programs.

The Contributions of Research

In this vein, the kinds of contributions that research *can* make should be noted. Research can provide us with new knowledge as well as test existing knowledge. It can hold our present assumptions up for scrutiny, giving us evidence concerning their truth or falsity. Research can be used to evaluate policies and practices. It can also be made an integral part of our experimental programs. For research to make these impressive contributions to education, however, requires fundamental changes in the kinds of research done. What *kind* of research is needed?

The Characteristics of Needed Research

A major need is for increased sophistication in the conceptualization, design, and conduct of research. What is termed "research" can vary considerably in rigor and utility. In examining this point, it is instructive to note Lundberg's well-known discussion of levels or methods of scientific procedure.[12] Lundberg identified four of these, the first being *random observation*. This simplest and crudest method of research consists of occasional and somewhat haphazard observations —"exploratory" studies. This method is sometimes called "radical empiricism" or "naked empiricism." It rests on faith that the "facts will speak for themselves," that their meaning will somehow become clear. It has become abundantly clear that this faith is unfounded. This method has its chief utility as a source of ideas for more advanced research.

The second level or method discussed by Lundberg consists of *systematic explorations of broad fields or subjects*. Its chief important difference from random observation is in the precision and care shown in data collection and analysis. This method remains valuable in research areas where existing knowledge is slight or poorly organized.

The *testing of well defined but isolated hypotheses*, either by experiment or statistical methods, is the next level. Here hypotheses are stated explicitly, data are gathered and analyzed to test them, and generalizations are formulated.

In terms of scientific sophistication, the fourth level is the most advanced. It consists of *research directed by systematic and integrated*

---

[12] George A. Lundberg, *Social Research*. New York: Longmans, Green and Co., 1942, pp. 5-9.

theory. "This method begins with (1) a set of rigorous and unambiguous terms to be used. (2) Next is stated a set of postulates or hypothetical statements and their corollaries (inferences from the postulates) which are tentatively assumed to be true for the purpose of the investigation. (3) Thirdly, theorems are stated as formal propositions which could or should be true if the postulates, the corollaries and the reasoning in the theorems are sound. These theorems are really hypothetical generalizations, which direct the nature of the (4) empirical observations undertaken to test the validity of the entire explicit theoretical structure outlined above."[13]

Lundberg's discussion provides a benchmark for the evaluation of research in education; it makes it possible both to see where we are and the directions in which we should seek to go. Clearly, the lion's share of research remains at the first two levels, with some studies now being attempted at the third. It is also clear that our goal should be to conduct virtually all research at the third and fourth levels eventually.

THE ROAD AHEAD

No one should underestimate the difficulty of reaching this goal. In moving in that direction, we must contemplate perhaps decades of struggling. We must not only train substantial numbers of researchers and disseminate research findings widely, but we have an even larger task, that of developing a respect for and sympathetic attitude toward research throughout the armies of educational practitioners. Otherwise, research will be of limited effectiveness. The development of a scientific perspective and a research orientation is the most urgent and important challenge facing those who are responsible for training programs at all levels.

In research training programs, we should banish radical empiricism, making investigations at this level no longer acceptable or respectable. Obviously, we should insist on methodological rigor. But this alone is not enough. Above all, perhaps, we should emphasize the nature and functions of theory in research. It must be reiterated that theory gives meaning to facts (i.e., points to the relationships among facts, to their ordering in a meaningful fashion).

We should also insist that claims to reliable knowledge must be of the sort that are capable of being tested (confirmed or rejected). The day of the unsupported generalization and the confident cliché should be brought to an end. We should be ever-ready to abandon our cherished assumptions and beliefs when evidence points in other directions. This self-corrective attitude has been rightly described as the most important characteristic of science. As Feigl has said, "It is a sign of

---

13 *Ibid.,* p. 7.

one's maturity to be able to live with an unfinished world view."[14]

I have tried in this paper to identify what our goals and procedures should be in our search for reliable knowledge. The road ahead is long and arduous. We will not and cannot change our traditional ways of doing things overnight. But we can look forward to the day when our policies, practices, and innovations rest on firmer bases than they do now.

[14] Herbert Feigl, "The Scientific Outlook: Naturalism and Humanism," in Herbert Feigl and May Brodbeck (Eds.), *Readings in the Philosophy of Science.* New York: Appleton-Century-Crofts, Inc., 1953, p. 13.

6

Seminar on
Change Processes
in the
Public Schools

A. SUMMARIES OF GROUP DISCUSSIONS
B. SUMMARY OF SEMINAR

Summaries of Group Discussions

Seminar on
Change Processes in the Public Schools
OCTOBER 14-16, 1964

Group A—MATTHEW B. MILES

We began our work by getting some underbrush out of the way, as I saw it. This centered around the problems of language (using words in special ways, jargon, not being simple and direct). We agreed that these were faults both of the behavioral sciences and of education, and we tried to install a ground rule that when somebody didn't understand something that he stop then and there and say "What do you mean?" We seemed to be able to use this rule relatively well.

We then launched into a discussion which kicked off with the idea (which I was advocating pretty strenuously) that we all have theories of operation, and theories of change. It is never a question of having no theory. All of us have ideas, guidelines, or a kind of framework of principles which guide our work. We began our discussion by trying to understand what some of the various personal theories around the group were.

We then looked at a series of aspects of change situations which various people around the table thought were crucial. Here is a list of these:

(1) Where the change comes from—is it external or internal to the system?

(2) The relative speed with which the change is introduced.

(3) Its timing, in relation to other changes or events in the system.

(4) The style of implementation; for example, does it need to be "grass rootsy" or is it possible that arbitrary imposition-type changes can also become installed?

(5) How dissatisfied people are with the status quo. Here again, we raised the question—"Is it necessary that people be dissatisfied in order for change to take place?"

(6) The role of curiosity and inquiry.

(7) Money and "forced compliance." I gave an example in which people had been paid to carry out changes; these changes not only

[79]

became installed but were accompanied by enthusiastic attitudes. This led in turn to the idea that having active experience with something new often changes the attitudes of acceptance radically.

(8) The general attitude toward innovation and change—favorableness or unfavorableness—existing in a particular organization.

At that point in our discussion, we focused very clearly, I felt, on the question of separating what actually occurs in an organization from our wishes, desires, or good-bad judgments about them. This led us into, not surprisingly, the role of the superintendent.

We worked for quite a while on various roles, in relation to change, which he might carry out. We ended up with four, and we hoped with each one to look at the consequences—that is, to get away from the idea that it is good to be "X" or bad to be "X." Rather, if you are "X," what are the results likely to be as far as the state of the organization and the change are concerned.

The first role was *content initiator*. Here, the superintendent says, for example, "I am for kindergarten." He may say this openly or in a closed or indirect way. Any one of these roles can be carried out explicitly, on the table—"I am for the introduction of kindergarten, and everybody knows it." Or one can be a content initiator indirectly, or covertly, in a closed, way.

The second role is *process initiator*. This role is not that of pushing hard on the content of the innovation, but that of actively setting plans in motion (e.g., setting up a committee that includes people from various levels of the system and the community to work on the issue of kindergarten). Here the superintendent is not taking a position on the content, but is trying to set a structure in motion which will let people, including himself, work on the problem.

The third role we talked about was that of *mediator*. Here the superintendent is not actively pushing either for content or for process, but to aid, in a sense, the initiative of other people (his assistant, building principals, somebody in the community or whatever). He is a kind of catalyst in which other people are doing the main content push, the main process push, but he is, in a sense, in a kind of mediating, facilitating kind of role.

The last role was *squasher*. You can openly or indirectly block an innovation by sitting on it, by saying "that's no good, it won't work," or by letting it be known that you think it won't work.

We didn't talk about the consequences of all of the roles, and we disagreed a lot, interestingly I thought, on what the consequences were. For example, it was pointed out that if you take the mediating role and the innovation is a success, other people get the credit. If it's a failure, it may still be your neck. Or, if you take the content innovating role saying "I am for kindergarten, and I think it's a good idea," the consequences in the case of success or failure, especially failure, may be fairly harsh. You have stuck your neck out, plumped for a particular thing, and it may be much harder to initiate other innovations in the future. We also talked about the "sneakiness" of the mediating role as a potential problem in terms of consequences.

Some other points were made about these roles. First, that one doesn't choose one of these four roles and apply it mechanically in all innovative situations. The problem facing the chief school executive is to look at a situation and select from this array of roles, behavior that will work, and that is compatible with his own durable style. It was pointed out that some people can't be mediators for the life of them; certain other people, if you asked *not* to be a content initiator, are under terrible tension—they've just got to give their opinions.

Secondly, we discussed the characteristics of the immediate task. Some curricular innovations might appropriately require a mediating style, for example, and it is possible that certain administrative innovations could be carried out essentially by content initiation. ("This is what we're going to do, and this is how I feel about it.")

We then closed with, I think, a couple of interesting ideas. We had been talking up to that point almost as if the superintendent were the key—as if he were the only person in the situation and as if his way of operating an innovative role was going to be the sole determinant of the consequences. The group began backing away and pointing out that there are figures called building principals and various other figures in the system, and that working with them turns out to be very crucial. Lastly, we came up with the idea that it would be fun to go back to our systems, make a check list of these four types of innovative roles, and ask our principals to fill it out, both in terms of "how you see me" and "how you would like me to behave," on different kinds of innovative issues.

Group B—EVERETT M. ROGERS

Group B this morning, focused most of our attention on promiscuous questions for research. I would like to list briefly these research questions suggested by the group.

1. We expressed a need for a national, and less than national, coordinating agency for educational research, a new agency (or perhaps some existing organization) that would produce syntheses of existing research studies, and future research studies, so that one is not faced with a multitude of individual research results which sometimes contradict each other. This would also be an agency that would, hopefully, give advice on implementation of research results at the local level.

2. The need for research to more clearly evaluate educational innovations was also stated. Granted that changes in education are sometimes difficult to evaluate, in a broad sense, we thought there was a need for research on, and resulting recommendation of, which innovations will give what results. We hope that this might tend to decrease the presence of "fads" in educational change.

3. The need for research on educational campaigns, particularly educational financial campaigns, was expressed. Such studies might be made, for instance, of why campaigns fail or why they succeed;

the use of, for instance, fear appeals and threat appeals in these campaigns and the informational nature involved in these campaigns; the presenting of one side versus two sides of issues in these campaigns; and, in general, an analysis of why is it, what is it, with some campaigns that make them succeed.

4. Research is needed on images of the role of school officials, particularly the chief school administrator. Why is it that school administrators (they feel) have low credibility in the eyes of the public? In other words, why is it that your populace doesn't trust you when you say something? The research question may be more properly framed by asking "What are the public images of the school official?" One reason for feeling that this question was important was that some school administrators thought that, on at least a few occasions, the populace, all of the populace, did not place complete credibility in what the school administrator said publicly.

5. I'm not really sure how to put it in a research question, but, in general, the question was—"Why is it (maybe there is an assumption here, too) that the public schools are a common object of frustration as expressed on the part of the public?" Or, put in farm boy language, "Why are schools dead horses that the public keeps kicking?" I guess really maybe the basic question is, "Is this true?"

---

*Group C—*James Q. Wilson

I asked the group to tell me what their guidelines are; their common sense rules of thumb; their proverbs, if you will, of good administration. We got quite a list, in fact, 17 items. There was, I think, considerable agreement that this was a representative list.

Then I pointed out, as the people who suggested these items were fully aware, that many of the items were mutually contradictory. I suggested that one way of indicating the degree to which they were contradictory was to divide them into two columns and to give as labels to these two columns, titles which were first given to such traits by the first theorist of administrative behavior and organizational decision-making—Nicolo Machiavelli. He wrote of the differences between the lion and the fox and the importance to the Prince of knowing when to be a lion and when to be a fox.

The fox-like traits, which are these days stated as "supportive," "participative" traits include the following:

Go slow! Don't make decisions rapidly. Gain the confidence of your staff and community or board. Be a good listener and a courteous listener. Try to understand different points of view, and different values. Don't try to get ahead of public opinion. Create a climate hospitable to innovations, suggestions and cooperation. Give recognition where recognition is due to the efforts of others.

Then, in the lion's column are such statements as:

Sometimes you have to be a leader. Sometimes you have to be courageous and take risks. Remember public memories are short.

Don't rely on public good will. Don't be afraid to move ahead. Sometimes you have to be decisive. Don't let people box you in. Be sure you have objectives, even if you don't state them to the community at large.

I think that these lists have two characteristics which I would like to mention very quickly. One is that this is essentially the same list that I get when I ask this question of business executives. This suggests to me how common the concerns are of administrators and how common the approaches to the solutions of these problems are.

The second comment I want to make is that most of the people acted as if they were always "eagle scouts." Although they did mention under both the list of lion-like traits and the list of fox-like traits many things which Machiavelli had suggested, they conspicuously failed to mention other things that were on his list such as flattery, cooptation, deceit, bribery. There was silence for a while, then some people in our group admitted this by saying, "Well, it is true that you can't always tell everybody all the truth all the time. When you're trying to respond to a parent's appeal to have his child assigned to teacher A, rather than teacher B, you can't always tell them that, indeed, teacher B is better than teacher A." You must sometimes follow "reasons of state" as Machiavelli said and for the good of the organization, conceal a bit of the full story. In giving recognition to people, you often have to give recognition where recognition is not due. Sometimes this comes pretty close to flattery.

The real problem, of course, is not how hygienic or how devious the items on this list may be. The real point is, "What can social science tell an administrator who formulates a list of guidelines which are internally inconsistent?" Is there anything that social science can suggest that would lead him out of this box? My position on this is that, by and large, there is not. There is a great deal of research needed to be done in education and in educational administration, and I encourage Oregon and anybody else to do good research. But, it seems to me, on this particular point—how you improve upon this list of proverbs—social science has relatively little to say. It has relatively little to say for two reasons. One is empirical, one logical.

Empirically, it is very easy to think of extraordinarily successful administrators who, to an extraordinary degree, embodied the lion-like characteristics almost entirely or the fox-like characteristics almost entirely. In the army, General George Patton ran the Third Army like a lion; General Eisenhower ran SHAEF headquarters like a fox. In the field of federal administration of public housing programs, Robert Moses of New York City ran the public housing program like a lion, his successors are now running it like a fox. (It's hard to tell who has been the most successful.)

The second problem, though, is more complicated. Not only is it easy to find good cases of lion-like leaders or fox-like leaders and not only is it hard to find convincing reasons for persuading lion-like leaders to be more fox-like and vice-versa, there are also certain logical problems that confront social science when it tries to help an administrator eliminate the inconsistencies, and thus, to know the circumstances under which to apply one rule rather than another. The reason for this is that social science attempts to produce propositional knowledge—generalized knowledge or generalizable knowledge about things that are true most of the time, to most of us, under most circumstances. It can state, for example, what the characteristics of populations are. It can give you the frequency distribution of attributes. It can tell you, not only how many people have red hair, black hair and blond hair, it can also tell you what is the distribution of I.Q., of political preferences, of teachability, of creative impulses. Social science can also generate propositional knowledge which has to do with the analysis of variance. It can try to explain what the effects are of changing a particular variable, or what the relationship is between two variables. But it can only do this under very special circumstances—when it has a relatively clear and unambiguous measure of what the effects are and when it can control the changes. In other words, it has to have a measure of output and it must have experimental control to deal with the problem of variance.

Now, this is useful knowledge for many purposes. It is most useful to a school superintendent, it seems to me, when the problem at hand depends on his knowing the characteristics of his pupil population, the sorts of things they will respond to, the distribution of attributes among them, the likely consequences of making certain changes in curriculum, etc. But my point, I feel, is that most of the time the superintendent doesn't concern himself with these matters. During only a small fraction of his time is he concerned with what the organization does, how it teaches kids, or how it contributes to the welfare of society. The superintendent, particularly in the small districts, spends most of his time on maintaining the organization—dealing with the board, the teachers, the community, conducting the organization's foreign affairs and managing its administrative problems. This often has little to do in a direct sense with educating children, although in the long run it has a great deal to do with it.

It is with respect to these problems that non-propositional knowledge is most important. What are the things that an administrator needs to know to be able to tell under what circumstances he should apply a rule from the lion list and under what circumstances he should apply a rule from the fox list? It seems to me, there are several things he needs to have. He needs to be a good guesser. He must have an ability to make probability estimates about unique events, not about how many times heads will come up if you flip a coin 50 times, but whether the school board chairman will take course A or course B.

Secondly, he must have a knowledge of the motives of people, but not people in general. Social science can tell him a great deal about the motives of people in general under certain circumstances. He needs to know the motives of a handful of people who may or may not fit certain general rules and propositions, and this is something he can learn only by direct experience—if indeed he can learn it at all.

Thirdly, he has to be able to make value judgments—"What ought we to do in this circumstance?"; "If I have to choose, what should I choose?" On this again, social science may indicate what, in the majority of cases, will be the consequences of certain alternatives, but usually the choice is so constrained, so narrow, between two such rather limited alternatives that this generalized knowledge isn't very valuable. He simply has to know, under the circumstances, which direction into the dark he should leap.

Fourth, he needs an analytical ability to find in the welter of detail, circumstance, personality, time, rhetoric and emotion, the crux of the issue. He must avoid details, or the periphery of the issue, but spend his time focusing his energies on the thing on which everything else depends. And again, social science also tells you in general terms on what certain outcomes depend. But, the school superintendent, like most administrators, is not dealing with general problems. He has to feel out for himself whether to apply a rule from the lion list or the fox list, just as he has to decide for himself under what circumstances generalized, propositional, social science knowledge is usable and under what circumstances he is dealing with a state of affairs which is the exception to the rule, which is not consistent with the kind of knowledge that social science has generated.

It seems to me, as we end the conference, we should not conclude that we ought to have a lot of research, or that every school superintendent should be research-oriented. We may take good administrators and make them into lousy social scientists. The kind of knowledge that research can give you may be very valuable depending on the kind of information you need to know. But I'm convinced from reading the questions that were on the list you submitted that few issues depend for their resolution upon propositional knowledge.

––––––––––

Group D—ART GALLAHER, JR.

In line with the general theme of the conference, "Change Processes in the Public Schools," we sort of indirectly arrived at two basic assumptions. One of these is, of course, that the school administrator can apply data in the form of innovations; secondly, that these data are primarily the product of research.

We then focused our attention on the problem of the "middle ground"—how to get the social scientist to communicate his data in a form that can be understood and applied by the school administrator; and, getting the school administrator to come to the middle ground in a way so that he can understand research data and transform them into innovations. The middle ground, then, lies between the scientist and the practitioner.

These were our concerns: First, with the general problem of relating the researcher and the practitioner, since innovation must rest on a body of basic knowledge; and secondly, with how this conference relates to this general problem of the middle ground, and with how successful we've been in developing some ability to communicate with and understand each other.

In terms of the first problem, that of getting research data to the practitioner, a number of conclusions were arrived at in our particular group. One is a criticism by the school administrators that practical problems are not researched enough; that they are forced, whether they want to or not, to rely upon common sense knowledge, that they have to "fly by the seat of their pants" for the most part; that the kinds of practical problems which the school administrator faces, and which he must have innovations to solve, are not really given enough research attention.

The second conclusion was that there is a lack of communication between those who do the research and those who are in positions to apply it. That is to say, there is a lack of communication in those areas where there are data that can be applied—it simply does not always get down to the unit of application. Some of the administrators pointed out that they get involved in research designs that emanate from the University and other places, but the results of this research seldom get back to them. In some cases it does, but more often they participate and give time in assembling data and that is the last they ever hear of it.

The recommendation, in terms of these two kinds of problems, by the administrators, is that researchers go into the field to design their projects; that researchers get into ongoing educational systems; that they consult more with school administrators about the kinds of practical data that are needed. The group was quite candid, too, in its admission that administrators are also at fault in this process. They say they have difficulty getting into the middle ground and that one of their main problems is that they are not sophisticated enough about research design and basic tools of research. There are other variables that are involved here—there is no point in mentioning many of them because they are the common kinds of problems that have come up here in practical ways throughout the whole meeting—such as the problem of time. For example, how does one get time to simply assemble the data of research?

There was also a fear expressed on the part of the administrators that research in education is becoming more sophisticated, and although this is a good thing, the people who have already "been through the mill" and who are out in the ongoing systems will find it increasingly difficult to understand the findings of such research. Thus, practitioners are going to be further removed from the middle ground than they already are. They see this as a definite problem of the future.

These are the major problems we talked about in trying to get together. We then turned our attention on how this conference, as one kind of vehicle—pilot that it is—has functioned in arriving at a middle ground. This was really our major concern.

I think one of the most significant suggestions made by the group is that there needs to be something of a decompression period before getting involved in the business of a conference. Most of the participants came immediately from their problems, their desks, and, it takes a while to really get into the swing of things. It might be a worthy proposition to consider having a couple of days free (a retreat or something like this) to study the papers. It is also felt that it might be a good idea to have an hour or two so that one can go through the paper (if he had studied it previously, of course) just before confronting the consultant.

It was felt, too, that some of the group dynamics sessions the first day tended to become too generalized. Both the participants and the consultants were blamed for this. The participants very often got so concerned with exchanging ideas on their own problems that they strayed too far from the central topic, and the consultants were not always as careful as they might have been in controlling the discussions.

These problems are only listed here because we can't go into their discussion. In ranging over them, however, a number of substantive sub-topics were brought up. For example, the question was raised whether or not the administrator is the crucial variable on which we could focus attention and direct a change in the internal system of the school. After all, the acceptance or rejection ultimately comes from the teacher. We raised the question (we didn't answer it) whether or not we should be focusing so much attention on the administrator. Certainly we questioned the assumption that administrators themselves can necessarily effect change.

Also the problem of role definition was brought up, especially the conflicting role images held by the various publics in the community that the school administrators must relate to. This, incidentally, is thought of as an area that needs considerable research. The problem of how to communicate to various segments of the public—how to maintain lines of communication. both formal and informal—was also a suggested topic for research. Finally, we discussed briefly the problems of research in ongoing school systems.

Summary of Seminar on
Change Processes in the Public Schools

DONALD E. TOPE
University of Oregon

I've developed my summary around four major points. Dick Carlson started us off on an important concept that should have been encouraging to you—that the administrator *does* make a difference. Some recent research points to the fact that how the administrator does act, how successful he is in his district, has a major impact on the education enterprise. This impact is over and beyond the availability of resources and point directly at the administrator and his administrative style of operation.

The second major point in summary, to me, was the extent to which we came to realize that the insights and knowledge of those who study human behavior, and human institutions is relevant to school administration. The prepared papers provided a great deal of interest, concern, and discussion pointing to the relevance that these concepts have to school administrators and to their operations.

The papers also provided a good deal of comparability, of agreement. There was the agreement that education in this country has a great deal of goal ambiguity and that this is an interfering factor in terms of trying to effect changes. Part of this ambiguity, of course, is due to the fact that there is the same kind of ambiguity in our society. We are a pluralistic society and any attempt to develop a definite set of agreements with regard to goals would probably be actually against the kind of society we have. Nevertheless, when a change is being considered, defining the goal is an important aspect of the change and the change process.

I think that there was general agreement with the notion of the diversity of the educational enterprise, the internal diversity within the establishment. This is not new to you, but our consultants emphasized the interference that this degree of diversity, the increased specialization in education has for effecting change. Such concepts as the *low interdependence* among people in the educational enterprise due to the fact that they have their own specific jobs; and *role invisibility*, the extent to which the teacher is not closely supervised, are factors to be taken into account in effecting change. Part of the challenge for the school administrator is that of providing some means for developing an adoption process when changes are being considered; a process which provides for discussion, a kind of forum where the criticisms about present practices can be brought into the open, where some opportunity to make evaluations can be induced or encouraged. Out of this kind of discussion, of bringing various elements within the educational enterprise into communication, we may be able to create a greater degree of interdependence. What may result is a recognition that a change in one aspect of the educational structure may indeed affect other elements in the structure.

I think you have been provided a great experience in how to use consultants effectively. Outside people have been recognized as offering one means by which change can be given some consideration in a school district. And, the way in which you utilize consultants from the outside is one of the means you have of bringing about at least the consideration of change.

There has been general agreement, it seems to me, that an important aspect of education is the lay-professional relationship—the importance of the client group to the schools and to the administrator. The client group provides the basis of support. Success in administration rests finally on group support for the enterprise. The administrator, I think, was given a very excellent precaution: that in serving the client group he would have to be very careful that he wasn't becoming subservient to it.

A fourth general agreement was the distinction between the administrator acting as the *advocate* for change and the administrator acting as a *mediator*. Involving himself as an advocate to the extent that he is inflexible in being able to see possibilities of adaptations in the suggestions for change, to see ways that might overcome some of the resistance to change, will reduce the effectiveness of the administrator. The concept of effecting change being political in nature brings a very important concept to the administrator. In recognizing himself as a politician in the best sense; in trying to bring about a situation where general support can be generated within the organization as well as in the external environment in which the school exists, the school administrator has his major role. We have throughout this seminar given recognition to the crucial role of the administrator in office. Because he is not setting himself up as the advocate in the change operation does not mean that he is less important. The role that he plays as a politician is still a most effective and most important one.

There was general agreement in thinking of the environment for change—both within the organization itself and external to the organization as a vital factor in change. Here, such things as the often mentioned need for a sense of timing comes into effect. Maybe we will not be able to research this point, maybe this is just not the kind of question that *can* be researched. The administrator still has to try to gauge this matter of environment to see when the proper timing is for announcing the change, for getting the motions, the arrangements, the machinery into action for the consideration of change. A sense of timing is an important ingredient in the whole change process.

There was general agreement, I think, on the importance of specifying the outcomes of change. Such agreement is one way in which some frustration, some misunderstanding can be avoided. If there is clear enunciation, a clear explication of the intended outcomes of a change, a better atmosphere for considering a proposed change is provided. It is well to keep in mind here, that being a domestic operation, the school doesn't have much in the way of profit motive to act as an inducement. Nevertheless, I think we can take some comfort in the fact that studies of job satisfaction indicate that the specific salary is not necessarily the important ingredient of job satisfaction. Other factors, paricularly those having to do with working relationships, human working relationships within the organization, stand even higher than the item of salary itself in job satisfaction. This is the kind of inducement that must be included in the objective of the change.

I think there has been agreement also in bringing our attention to the fact that there is increasingly a concern for the larger environment of education. Perhaps we have been too insular in thinking of the school primarily as a community operation. We are beginning to be reminded more and more that the major decisions are being made at the state and the national level. We must become more alert and more sensitive to the national interest. We must be alert and alive to the happenings that are occurring in the larger society which affect the school. In this connection, I was reminded that it is important for the school administrator today to change his reading habits so that he becomes conversant with some of the happenings in the larger society. There must be improved communication which will give the local administrator a better sense of the national picture. The importance of travel as one of the ingredients in change needs recognition. You, as the administrator, must become more and more the cosmopolite in your concern and understanding of the relationships of the school and the society of which it is a part.

Well, the third general item of my summary is this whole concept of the need for research, presented most effectively by Dr. Pellegrin last evening, and also in the kind of summary that was given to us this morning. There are several aspects of this, it seems to me, that have been brought out during this seminar. One of the problems which must be solved is the awareness on the part of the administrator, of research that has been carried out, as well as that which is under way. This, it seems to me, points definitely in the direction of an in-service program for school administrators. I think Dean Jacobson mentioned many times to you that his understanding of what's happening in the field of medicine is relevant here. Dean Baird of the University of Oregon Medical School claims that more money in his budget is spent now on in-service programs for physicians than in pre-service preparation programs. We may well be looking forward to this kind of a change in the expenditure of resources for preparation of school administrators. This seminar is, indeed, one example of our trying to find better ways of developing in-service programs with you. I think that it is significant that, in the initial planning of this seminar, there was consultation with your executive group.

Another aspect of this emphasis on research is the extent to which you can participate in studies; the extent to which you can encourage research going on in your district. In many respects you may need assistance on the part of this over-all state program in research, but I'm sure that much effort will be carried on in your district—if it's to be viable and meaningful in the operation of schools.

Another aspect of this research effort is your willingness to be studied. I don't think we'll be able to get very far in our studies of administration and the administrative process unless we are actually welcomed into your operation. We've been delighted in our research since the early days of CPEA to get the kind of cooperation that we have in Oregon. This is due to your willingness to become "guinea pigs," as it were, and allow yourselves to be studied.

Another aspect of this interest in research is the increased availability of money for research, particularly research having to do with certain kinds of innovative practices and their adoption at the district level. The school administrator is going to have to recognize the necessity of being alert and alive to the possibilities of getting some of these funds available in his district for research activities.

Well, fourth, and the final part of my summary is a little look into the future. Until we have research that gives us an unusual degree of understanding and confidence in the results about administration and about educational administration, we have to recognize that in many critical decisions, "you're damned if you do, and damned if you don't." The thing that I got out of the case that was discussed yesterday was that, in such situations, you're better off being damned for doing the thing that your experience, your training, your professional commitments indicate to you is the better of the alternatives provided. Your professional reputation is the thing at stake.

But, having said this, I recognize that in administration you need some luck, and so, in bringing a benediction to this experience, this seminar, let me close with that—may good fortune attend you!

Participating School Officials

Milt Baum

Willard Bear

Elliott Becken

Walter Commons

Kenneth Erickson

Fred L. Esvelt

Russell M. Esvelt

Wayne Foster

George M. Henderson

Bernard Hughes

Edwin T. Ingles

J. W. King

Hauton Lee

William E. Lewellen

R. La Verne Marcum

Clyde Martin

Nathaniel H. Moore

M. L. Morey

Ellis H. Neal

Douglas Olds

Henry O. Pete

Owen O. Sabin

Joe H. Stewart

William E. Stewart

Ken Stuart

John Thrasher

Nile G. Williams

Thomas E. Woods

Marlen D. Yoder